Baja California Sur

*An Expat's Relocation Guide for La Paz,
Cabo San Lucas, San José del Cabo, Los
Barriles, Mulegé, Todos Santos, and Loreto*

Expatriate and Escape the Rat Race!

An Expat Fever™ Series Book

Baja California Sur

An Expat's Relocation Guide for La Paz, Cabo San Lucas, San José del Cabo, Los Barriles, Mulegé, Todos Santos, and Loreto

Author: Manny Serrato

Note: No website or company has paid a fee in order to be mentioned in this book. All the information in this book is intended for educational purposes only and cannot be considered legal advice. Expats and those considering expatriation should consult professional legal and tax advisors if they have any questions.

Editors: Sarah Driffill and Elena N. Steele

In our candid interviews with local residents, all the names have been changed.

So You Want to Move to Baja California? Relocation Guide for La Paz, Cabo San Lucas, San José del Cabo, Los Barriles, Mulegé, Todos Santos, and Loreto

ISBN: 978-1-937361-45-7

Find out more about Expat Fever at our official website: www.expatfever.com.

More Expat Fever Books

Expat Fever Relocation Guides

*So You Want To Move To **Playa Del Carmen**?*

*So You Want To Move To **Tulúm**?*

*So You Want to Move to Baja **California Sur?*** *Relocation Guide for La Paz, Cabo San Lucas, San José del Cabo, Los Barriles, Mulegé, Todos Santos, and Loreto*

"Interview with an Expat" Information Guides

*Interview with an Expat: **Playa Del Carmen, Mexico**: Learn About the Mayan Riviera from Real Expats!*

*Interview with an Expat: **Tulúm, Mexico**: Learn About the Mayan Riviera from Real Expats!*

*Interview with an Expat: Costa Rica: Learn About **Costa Rica** from Real Expats!*

Table of Contents

Our Immigration Journey 9

Interview with Our Mexican Immigration Attorney 12

Common Questions that Apply to Everyone 17

La Paz: A Busy Capital City with a Beautiful Waterfront 24

Cabo San Lucas: Tourism and Nightlife 38

San José del Cabo: The Calmer Side of Cabo 56

Todos Santos: Artsy and Artisanal 80

Los Barriles: A Sport Fisherman's Paradise 91

Mulegé: A Natural Oasis with a Lush Prehistoric History 103

Loreto: Safety, Community, and Old World Grace and Charm 112

Reference Information for Local Schools 121

About the *Expat Fever* Series 139

Are You Ready for a Major Lifestyle Change?

The *Expat Fever* series is designed to give readers a candid view of what life is like for expats living overseas. The series is also meant to provide useful advice for those considering living in another country and is written from the perspective of real expats, who know exactly what the process of expatriation is like.

This particular book discusses Baja California Sur (BCS). Specifically, it covers the cities of La Paz, Cabo San Lucas, San José del Cabo, Los Barriles, Mulegé, Todos Santos, and Loreto.

In today's world, expatriating is now a realistic option for many people, and one of the most popular destinations for expats is Mexico. With so many people moving to Mexico, there must be something special about it!

Europeans, Canadians, and Americans are flocking to Mexico for a number of reasons. Some go for the warmer weather, while others are attracted by its close proximity to their country of origin. According to Mexican immigration statistics, more than 5 million expats are estimated to be living permanently in Mexico.

In the last two decades, Baja California Sur has become a premier vacation spot for people looking to enjoy beautiful beaches, great food, and a relaxed atmosphere—without spending a fortune! Many tourists find themselves falling in love with the region and decide to settle down for good in Baja California Sur.

Moving abroad is a daunting task. Besides the official paperwork, like obtaining a visa to live and work in Mexico, you must weigh the pros and cons of picking up everything and moving to another country to start a new life.

How much will it cost? Will I be able to make a living there? How will the move affect my children? These are important questions you need to be able to answer. Whatever their individual reasons, more and more people are leaving their homes and their jobs behind to start new lives in BCS. If you are interested in following in their footsteps to start a new life in paradise, but aren't quite sure how to get there, then just keep reading!

Our Immigration Journey

Housing! Bank accounts! Residency! These are the three main topics we get asked about all the time. Well, this first section is designed to answer your general questions about how to apply for Mexican residency. This process is the same all over Mexico. These are the main questions we get asked all the time.

Well, this first section is designed to answer general questions about how to apply for Mexican residency. Although it can be a time consuming process, it's not necessarily difficult. We chose to use an attorney to obtain residency for ourselves and our children. It made the whole process easier and it was relatively affordable (less than $500 for the attorney's fees in addition to the actual application costs, which were a few hundred dollars).

We have travelled and lived in many areas of Mexico. Mexico allows you to stay in the country as a tourist for up to 6 months without any issue. Since we traveled back to the U.S. frequently for business, we never felt pressured to obtain permanent residency.

But this year, we decided to make our residency official by going through the formal immigration process. *Starting* the process was easy, but *finishing* it was rather difficult, due to the bureaucratic red tape we encountered when we tried to complete the final steps in Mexico. After four repeated trips to the Mexican immigration office (there was always one little detail or piece of paperwork that we seemed to miss), we looked for an attorney to help us.

Mexican Immigration Office in Cabo San Lucas
(This is where we went to get my wife's Permanent Residency Card, with the help of our attorney).

We were very lucky to find an excellent immigration attorney (he also specializes in property and real estate contracts, which is a plus for anyone who wants to purchase property).

He fixed our nagging paperwork problem and even went to the immigration office to pick up our permanent residency card *in person!* Excellent service for a great price, which was about $350 total, including the initial consultation! Considering that our U.S. attorney charges us this amount **per hour**, it was an incredible bargain for the amount of aggravation he saved us.

The next section is our interview with Mr. Chávez, and his advice for our readers regarding Mexican immigration and other legal issues that are common for expats.

Interview with Our Mexican Immigration Attorney

LIC. Eduardo Chávez Fregoso
Real Estate and Immigration Attorney
eduardofregoso@yahoo.com
Plaza Centenario Local #3, Colonia Centro
Calle Manuel Doblado Esq. Blvd. Mijares
San José del Cabo, BCS México 23400
Baja California SUR

Manny: *Some Americans who want to obtain Mexican residency are confused about the process on how to do it. What would you recommend to them if they are not married to a Mexican citizen? What would be the process to obtain it? Is it true that the foreigner has to start the process in his/her country?*

Eduardo: *They have to start the process in any Mexican Consulate in their home country first. Now, the easiest way to start this process (if you are not married to a Mexican citizen or have Mexican citizen parents) is proving that you have enough money in your bank account to qualify for the income thresholds. Foreigners have to take care of a number of things in order to obtain Mexican residency.*

Steps to Get Permanent Residency in México

The first step is to contact the nearest Mexican Consulate in your home country. We did this in Sacramento, CA. The process was relatively easy and took less than a few hours.

Ask for an appointment to get a visa so you can get your "Temporary Residency Visa" in Cabo. Tell them that you will go for the "Economic Solvency" or "Bank Account Savings Visa"; that means that you have to prove that you have enough money in your bank account to live in Mexico, but tell them that you want to live or stay in Mexico for more than 6 months every year, because if you tell them that it will be for less time, they will not authorize it.

A "Temporary Residency Visa" allows you to stay in the country beyond the limits of the 6-month tourist visa and it allows you to obtain employment, open a bank account, and purchase real estate.

At your appointment, bring your original American or Canadian passport, two passport photos, and your last twelve bank statements. Your bank statements have to show a balance of $1,500.00 USD per month as minimum per person. This is relatively easy to achieve for couples on Social Security, or people who work online of have regular jobs with direct deposit.

If everything goes well at the meeting, they will glue a plastic visa in your passport, the same that you will have to show to Immigration upon your arrival at Cabo airport, or at the Immigration Office in Tijuana if you are driving down; in both cases, Immigration is going to give you a document that will allow me to start your residency process in Cabo.

Contact me as soon as you get your visa from the Mexican Consulate located in your country. I will review it and let you know the required materials that you will need to bring to continue with your residency process.

Permanent residency or temporary residency in Mexico is especially important for foreigners who want to own property in Mexico or get a job. The process is easier if you are related to a Mexican citizen or someone with existing legal Mexican residency.

Obtaining permanent residency or temporary residency gives you the right to stay in the country for over 180 days, get your CURP (Clave Única de Registro de Población, which is equivalent to the Social Security number in the U.S.), and, in some cases, gives you the right to buy or sell property.

You can open a Mexican bank account, get a driver's license, and if you want to work independently or open a business, it gives you the right to obtain your RFC (Registro Federal de Contribuyentes) Federal Taxpayer Registration.

Manny: *Many foreigners come to México and want to buy property. What is the main problem that they face if they are not well-informed at the moment of buying property? What would you recommend to avoid common pitfalls?*

Eduardo: *The most important thing to do is to notarize the sales contract immediately as they acquire the property. Many brokers advise them not to notarize, saying it is best to wait until they sell the property so they can save those expenses. In the U.S., a notary is usually present automatically when you purchase a home, but this is not always the case in Mexico. Not notarizing your contract properly can generate problems. If the original owner dies or his property later gets seized for some past debt, it makes it almost impossible for the foreigner to sell that property or recover what he has invested. The most important thing is to protect yourself.*

Also, it is recommended to notarize at the agreed price, never less, because when they sell their property in the future, they will have to pay a higher income tax or capital gains tax.

It is always advisable to hire the services of a lawyer closer (LER Closing Services), because there are many legal issues arising from the sale that the buyer has to be aware of, so the buyer gets what he bought and this can prevent problems in the future.

Manny: Thank you, Eduardo, for your great advice and feedback!

You can find the Mexican Immigration office in Cabo San Lucas

Lázaro Cárdenas 1625, Col. Centro C.P. 23410 Cabo San Lucas, B.C.S, Hours of Operation: Mon-Fri 9:00AM to 1:00PM.

Common Questions that Apply to Everyone

Here are the answers to the most common questions we receive about expatriating to Baja. These are real questions asked by potential expats, and we have duplicated our answers to them here.

1. Our family is seriously considering a move to Baja and are weighing our options. We want a family-friendly location and we plan to rent for at least a year. A 3BR/2BA works and if there's a small office in there, too, that would be a nice bonus. We are hoping to find a nice place for $2,000 or less (preferably a detached home). Do you think this is possible?

Manny's Answer: Absolutely, for that price range you can find a single-family home in a nice neighborhood. You can also find a nice condo on the beach for that price, although it won't be detached, and you'll have neighbors very close to you, (obviously).

The method we used all over Baja was to rent a nice place for a month using Airbnb, and then we took our time and searched for long-term rentals at a nice, unstressful pace. In some places, we just continued to rent using Airbnb and racked up airline miles on our credit card. By the end of the year, we had enough airline miles for free round trip airfare back to the US for our entire family. Gotta think outside the box!

The average rent (currently) for a nice 2-bedroom is about $900-$1,500 in an upscale community if that's what you want. It would be fairly easy to get a larger detached home for 2K. You can easily find studios and smaller apartments for less than $500 a month if you want to rent something small and save money while you decide on a permanent home.

Our advice: stay away from Cabo Bello (a planned community in the Corridor). Cabo Bello has serious water problems and residents there frequently go without water for several days. Research any other properties thoroughly before you sign a lease. In some of those areas, the owners are DESPERATE to sell or rent to anyone that will take a property off their hands. You can also rent a hotel for a week or so, but we like having a full kitchen and a laundry room so we rarely do that. And, no matter what you do, do NOT rent or buy anything for long-term until you see it in person.

2. Our son is in elementary school and will start the equivalent of 4th grade next year. I want my kid in an environment where learning Spanish is a big part of their education. What is the process to enroll my child in school?

Manny's Answer: Our 10 year old is in currently enrolled in a bilingual private school and it is *wonderful*. If this was the only reason for us to come to Mexico, everything else being equal, we would have done it. We originally lived in California, where private school tuition was prohibitively expensive. The public school in Sacramento that our son was in was underfunded and crime-ridden. We couldn't afford thousands of dollars a month for a private school, and his public school was awful. We found coming to Mexico has been a godsend in terms of education for our child.

There are lots of private schools in Baja to choose from. You don't need Mexican residency to enroll your child in a Mexican private school. You will need a copy of their passport, their birth certificate, as well as school records showing the last year that they completed.

I suggest visiting a few and checking their class sizes, as well as how many teachers they have that speak both English and Spanish. When we visited our son's private school for the first time, the director came out to meet us personally and two of the teachers spoke to us in perfect English.

Coming to Mexico has allowed us to put our child in a modern private school with small classrooms. Affordable, too, compared to CA where we are from. Private schools are excellent in Mexico, and extremely affordable. This is true even for children who have special educational needs. Our eldest is currently in a prestigious bilingual private school for about $250 USD a month, after an initial fee of about $600. That price included materials and books.

Class sizes are small in Mexican private schools. Our son's school has a modern computer lab. They even offer a robotics class! This has been a wonderful experience for us, after not being able to afford private schools in the US and pulling our children out of an awful, underfunded public school. (Please note that at the publication of this book, the peso is currently hovering at around 20: 1 to the US dollar, which means our dollars stretch much further). However, even if the peso were to stabilize later this year, private school in Mexico would still average about $400 per month. This is less than a third of the average cost of private school in the US.

3. What should we do with our vehicles? How hard is it to get Baja plates for our American cars?

Manny's Answer: I'll give you my opinion on this. As for cars, we didn't bother trying to legalize our used American cars. We bought a used Excursion down here for a couple thousand bucks. In our opinion, used cars are so cheap that it's not even worth it to transfer an American car and deal with the paperwork and the hassle. We sold our newer Avalanche in the US at Carmax they cut us a check the same day and that was it. We used that money to purchase a used car in Mexico with Mexican plates.

There are English-speaking insurance agents in Cabo who draft special permits for expats who want to bring their American cars down, but we didn't use those services because we discovered it would be approximately the same cost as buying a used car.

There are also regular dealerships like you can find in the US. Nissan, Mazda, Ford, and Toyota all have dealerships in Baja and you can certainly purchase a new car or a used car from a dealer just the way you would purchase one in the US or Canada.

If you want to legalize your American car, be aware that you can only legalize *certain years* (new American cars cannot be legalized with Mexican plates). This law changes frequently. HOWEVER, you can certainly bring your car down and drive it for approximately 6 months (or 180 days, the length of a tourist visa) while you decide what you want to do. So, you don't have to decide immediately. You can certainly use your own American car for a few months while you get settled, that will save you the money on a rental car. But be aware that you might have to drive it back to dump it in the US when the 180 days are over. The problem with having American license plates is that you also become a target for the police. Better to stay under their radar. That being said, we *personally* haven't had any issues. Not even theft. Los Cabos is very safe overall.

4. I'm an American and I want to move to Baja and work in the tourist industry there. What is terminology when we go down to stay permanently? Are we obtaining dual citizenship? Or are we just applying for residency?

Manny's Answer: For this scenario, you will be applying to become a legal Mexican RESIDENT. You can't just become a Mexican citizen right off the bat, unless you have a Mexican parent or grandparent. So, you will be applying for the Mexican equivalent of a "green card" in the US.

This will allow you to stay in Mexico indefinitely, work for a Mexican employer, buy property and open a bank account. You won't be able to become a Mexican citizen until you are living in Mexico for at least a few years. Then, you can apply for citizenship and become a dual citizen if you want. You will not be relinquishing your American citizenship unless you want to, and to do that you have to go to a US consulate and formally renounce as well as pay a fee.

5. What should we do about bank accounts?

Manny's Answer: We do not have Mexican bank accounts because of the onerous FATCA reporting requirements, which is a legal requirement for Americans to report foreign bank accounts. Rather than deal with that hassle, we obtained an HSBC bank account. We drove all the way to Oakland CA in order to get it, because HSBC is all over Mexico and since it's a US-based account, we don't have to pay any ATM fees or have any reporting requirements when we withdraw. Santander is another bank in Mexico that also has US branches (several in New York and New Jersey). We also retained our US-based Wells Fargo account and that's how we pay our US bills when we have to.

6. And we want to use our cellphone here as well as internet. What do you recommend?

Manny's Answer: For internet, we always make sure that we rent places that have free wi-fi. This has not been a problem as DSL internet service is now common all over Mexico. However, we also invested in a KeepGO device, which is a mobile 3G hotspot that works all over Mexico as well as other countries. It's metered, so data is expensive, but we use is only when we absolutely need to and it has helped us numerous times when wi-fi was unavailable.

For cellphones, we use Cricket as our cellphone provider. We have a family plan. Two of our family members in America use their phones up there, while we use our two cellphones in Mexico. It's a flat $150 per month for all 4 lines. The phones work in the US *as well* as Mexico so we always have cellphone service when we come back to the US on business. It works out great and there are no "surprise" fees like there is with AT&T and Verizon. After getting hit with a huge thousand-dollar "foreign roaming" bill with Verizon, we switched to Cricket. No more nasty surprises after that, we always know what our bill will be.

We are not affiliated with any of these companies, we are just letting our readers know what has worked for us. If you find something else that works for you, that's great.

La Paz: A Busy Capital City with a Beautiful Waterfront

The first place we visited in Baja California Sur was La Paz, the state capital. For us, the main highlight of La Paz was the waterfront promenade, or *El Malecón,* as it is called by the locals. This spectacular pedestrian walkway and strip of swimmable beaches is the city's main attraction, a must-see for anybody visiting La Paz.

The Malecón offers wide sidewalks (wide enough for bicyclists and roller skaters to use), beautiful local artwork, and benches just a few feet from the ocean, and many other attractions along the way. People often ride their bikes and go for walks here. Many of the residents we spoke with said the city's gorgeous waterfront was the primary reason they chose to live in this area.

A street view of "El Malecón", the waterfront pathway that spans several miles

La Paz is the political center of the region, as well as an important commercial center in its own right. You can enjoy beautiful sunsets, a myriad of water activities, and the authentic feel of a city that has yet to lose its charm to huge skyscrapers and thousands of tourists.

La Paz has a population of about a quarter-million residents. The city is full of people from all walks of life and boasts great hospitals, many schools, and a number of restaurants, bars, and shops. Life in La Paz is laid-back, but never dull. There is plenty to do here, and the beach is only a short drive away from any area of the city.

If you're looking for a city full of beautiful scenery without the resort town feel, La Paz may just be the place for you and your family to settle down in Mexico.

Location, Population, and Size

La Paz is about a two-hour drive from Cabo San Lucas and San José del Cabo, (also called "Los Cabos") the two major resort towns in Baja California Sur. La Paz located along the Gulf of California, also known as the *Sea of Cortez.*

There are noticeably fewer tourists in La Paz than the Cabo region. Our impression of the city was that there was much more "hustle and bustle", as well as active businesses.

La Paz has a major shipping port. In Los Cabos, we saw cruise ships filled with tourists, but in La Paz, the harbor is filled with huge cargo ships carrying automobiles and other goods instead. La Paz does see its share of tourists, but much of the tourism in La Paz comes from within Mexico itself. For example, when we visited the beaches in La Paz, we met several tourists from other areas of Mexico, but not a single tourist from outside the country. This was in stark contrast to ever other city that we visited.

Overall, La Paz has a much different feel from most of BCS. In some respects, this is a positive thing. Local residents can walk along the Malecón boardwalk without being bombarded with massive hotel skyscrapers, pushy street vendors, and all-inclusive resorts.

Points of Interest in La Paz

Although there is a small tourist area and several upscale hotels, La Paz is a relatively quiet. Many of the older buildings in La Paz reflect the city's colonial past, giving the town a charming aesthetic.

Eco-tourism is a major attraction in La Paz because of its location by the Sea of Cortez, where more than 85% of marine mammals in the Pacific and 35% of the marine mammals in the world can be spotted.

You can also enjoy a variety of aquatic activities, including scuba diving, snorkeling, kayaking, canoeing, whale watching between the months of October and March, and whale shark watching between the months of December and February. If you're an avid fisher, you can also join fishing charters and tours.

We went snorkeling several times on Balandra Beach and Tecolote Beach, two lovely beaches that are popular with the locals and are located about 25 minutes from La Paz.

The water was clear and beautiful. You could easily spot large schools of fish and other marine life.

Kayakers enjoying the water in La Paz

Balandra Beach is an especially good place to take your children to go swimming. The water here is relatively shallow. You can walk about 50 yards out and the water will only be about five feet deep.

If you go to Balandra Beach, take some time to see El Hongo (the famous "mushroom") as well. It's a popular spot along Balandra Beach. To get there, you have to walk from the parking lot along the beach to reach it. It's about a ten-minute walk, but well worth it.

"El Hongo" the famous "Mushroom" a natural landmark balancing rock formation that attracts thousands of tourists each year

La Paz: The Pros

Residents in La Paz enjoy some of the highest standards of living in Mexico. The average daily wage in La Paz is $27 USD, while the average daily wage countrywide stands closer to $16 USD. Because of its location, La Paz's economy does not rely as heavily on the tourism industry. Because it's the capital of Baja California Sur, many residents can find employment here through the government. This is a great area for expats who are bilingual, and since it's the capital, there is plenty of work that does not revolve around the unpredictable nature of the tourist industry.

The city's close proximity to the Sea of Cortez also makes La Paz a prime location for scientists and marine biologists. Many of them choose to work in eco-tourism or at universities.

Many of La Paz's landmarks have been reconstructed in the past couple of decades. This not only makes the city more attractive for potential visitors, it also improves the quality of life of local residents.

The Malecón is one of these reconstructed areas. This boardwalk spans several miles and boasts many different restaurants, shops, and bars. Much of the social life in La Paz centers around the boardwalk. Locals visit the restaurants and bars to enjoy a meal or a round of beers. Local businesspeople also conduct meetings at the boardwalk over breakfast or lunch. In the evening, you can see joggers taking in the scenery and enjoying the captivating sunsets.

You can also take a walk along the boardwalk to soak up the culture of La Paz. Sculptures by famous Mexican artists like Juan Soriano and Rocio Sanchez line the boardwalk. The favorites among the locals are *El Viejo y el Mar* by Guillermo Gomez and *La Ballena* by Octavio Gonzalez.

Piers for eco-tourism cruises can be found along the Malecón boardwalk. These tours will take you out on the water to enjoy the incredibly vast array of ocean wildlife that can be found in the Sea of Cortez.

La Paz's nightlife also centers around the Malecón. While La Paz isn't as well-known for its clubs or bars as Cabo San Lucas, there are several popular bars and nightclubs for people to enjoy on the weekends.

Velasco Garden, which has also been renovated in recent years, serves as the city's square, with many restaurants and stores to shop at. These squares are called *zócalo* in Mexico. Velasco is shaded by trees and a fountain is located in the center of the square.

This square acts as a meeting place for locals and visitors. Several of La Paz's cultural events, including dancing and book fairs, take place in Velasco Garden. The square also contains various historical buildings, like the *Catedral de Nuestra Señora de la Paz* (Cathedral of Our Lady of Peace) and the old *Palacio del Gobierno* (Governor's Palace). The library of the Regional History of California is located in the Governor's Palace.

La Paz: Cons

La Paz has everything that you might expect from any capital city—lots of modern amenities and entertainment, including modern architecture, shops, museums, and services. There are also negatives that come with any large city, such as additional traffic, visible poverty, pollution, and crime. There is also some drug-related violence.

According to the Department of Interior of Mexico, Baja California Sur registered its highest homicide rate ever in October 2015. The majority of these homicides occurred in La Paz, where there has been an increase in public acts of violence between rival criminal gangs. The violence settled down again in 2016, but the warning remains.

We saw no evidence of this violence during our visit to La Paz. Like any major city, drug-related crimes usually occur in the slums, and the police do everything they can to keep tourists and expats safe. In our experience, we never felt unsafe in La Paz, but we avoided the poorer areas of the city and stayed mostly around the waterfront.

During our visit to La Paz, we saw beautiful, unspoiled beaches, gorgeous golf courses, and luxury shops. We also saw homeless people begging in the streets or by the waterfront and quite a lot of graffiti. There are definitely "wealthy areas" and "poor areas" in La Paz, and the contrast seemed greater here than any other city that we visited in Baja.

For those readers who are familiar with California, it reminded us a bit of Santa Cruz, which also has a beautiful beachfront boardwalk, but is plagued by many of the same issues: a large homeless demographic, as well as a fair number of aggressive panhandlers living in the downtown area. Santa Cruz also has a graffiti and petty theft problem that goes hand-in-hand with poverty. Use common sense when you visit these parts of the city. Lock things up and don't leave your children or belongings unattended.

Living like a Local in La Paz

La Paz has grown and changed a lot over the years. Thirty years ago, farmers and ranchers filled the streets of La Paz. Today, the majority of the population in La Paz consists of young professionals with families, travelers and tourists, and retired couples. According to the Washington Post, La Paz currently boasts the highest concentration of Mexicans with PhDs. The population hovers at around 250,000, including approximately 6,000 permanent residents from the United States and Canada. We encountered many fluent English speakers while we were there, as well as a fair number of people who also spoke French.

Compared to other cities in BCS, there are fewer tourists in La Paz, so it may be more difficult to find information about homes, schools, and everyday life on the internet in English. This fact isn't necessarily a "con", because it gives you the opportunity to connect with locals and immerse yourself in real Mexican culture. Just be aware that you should commit to learning the language if you want to live in in La Paz permanently.

The Weather: Pros and Cons

La Paz is ecologically diverse. There are deserts, mountains, and plains in-between the Pacific Ocean to the west and the Sea of Cortez to the east. You can hike or bike up the mountains to see gorgeous panoramic views of La Paz, the Sea of Cortez, and the vast desert area of Baja, full of large cactus, ancient laurel trees, and coconut palms. The clear, blue waters of the Sea of Cortez are home to some of the most diverse populations of sea creatures in the world.

La Paz has a desert climate and is usually dry and hot. With over 300 days of sunshine during the year, average temperatures throughout the year range from 75-91°F. The summer months (between July and September) are the hottest and the most humid, with temperatures averaging around the mid-90s. In the winter months (December – February), temperatures average between 68 and 77 °F with night temperatures around 59 °F. Water temperatures in La Paz range from 68 °F in the winter and 85 °F during the summer months. The ocean here is comfortable for swimming all summer long and well into the fall.

Fortunately, the bay protects the city from seasonal storms coming in from the Gulf of California. Breezes from *Bahía de La Paz* moderate the temperature. The Coromuel winds, a weather phenomenon unique to the region, blow from the Pacific Ocean into the Bay of La Paz and cool the air on hot summer nights.

While we were in La Paz, it was hot, but not uncomfortably so. On the hottest days, we went to the beach, slathered on the sunscreen, and enjoyed the water. The evenings were always cool and we didn't need to use air conditioning at night. It didn't rain at all when we were there. Rainfall is rare during the most of the year, though there can be occasional erratic downpours. Most of the rain falls between the months of August and September.

Cost of Housing: Pros and Cons

The cost of housing in La Paz is significantly lower than any beachside property you'll find in the United States and Canada. There are many homes available for rent right near the waterfront for $500 – $750 USD. A sea-view, two-bedroom, two-bath home could cost as little as $1,000 a month. Prices are even lower for those who don't mind living a little further inland.

If you're looking to buy a place in La Paz, condos and houses close to the Sea of Cortez range wildly in price (depending on location), but you should be able to find a nice home for around $100,000 USD. Homes located right on the beach will be more expensive, and some areas (especially near the golf course or other "wealthy" zones) could cost up into the millions.

Make sure that your paperwork–this includes your residency visa–is in order before you consider purchasing, or even renting, a home. Beware of people who may try to take advantage of your lack of knowledge of the area or the language. Do your research about the prices of homes in the area and the process of owning a home in Mexico.

Many of the homes for rent and for sale are not advertised online. The internet only provides an introduction to the area and prices for houses and condos in La Paz. You will need to actually visit La Paz to get a better idea of the real estate available in the area and which areas of the city interest you the most.

Most of all, do not attempt to purchase *any* property in La Paz (or anywhere in Mexico, for that matter) unless you actually *see* it first. Timeshare scams are rampant all over Mexico, especially in the tourist zones. Therefore, you should avoid anyone who wants to give you a free breakfast or free dinner in exchange for going to a "short meeting".

Many scammers also exist on Craigslist and vrbo.com, and these should be avoided. Do *not* wire money to anyone you don't know. If it sounds "too good to be true", it probably is. If you see a super-cheap beachfront property, but the owner only accepts Western Union or cash wire transfers, that's your cue to run.

Our suggestion? The first time you visit, rent a nice hotel suite through a reputable company or use Airbnb and choose a host with good existing reviews. Do your research "on the ground" so you can see everything with your own eyes before you make any major decisions.

Pay for everything with a credit card (not a debit card, if you can help it!). That way, all your purchases are protected by your credit card policy and any fraudulent charges can be easily reversed, if necessary. This has saved us multiple times in Mexico.

Vendors are much more likely to honor their guarantees when there is a real possibility that they will be forced to issue a refund.

Employment for Expats: Pros and Cons

La Paz offers a large variety of employment options for expats who do not want to work in the tourism industry. You can seek a position at one of the many schools and universities. You may also be able to find work teaching English in a school or as a private tutor.

Many of the PhD-holders and government officials who work in La Paz hire tutors who speak English as their first language to teach English to them or their children. If you are a marine biologist or are highly-educated in any field, you can also look for a place in one of the universities.

If you don't *mind* working with tourists, eco-tourism is a thriving business in La Paz because of its close proximity to the Gulf of California. You can work for a fishing charter or eco-tourism business, or you can start your own. Always make sure that your residency papers are in order before you try to get a job or start your own business in Mexico.

It can be difficult to find well-paying work in Mexico if you aren't a highly-skilled worker. If you cannot find a job with an already established company, you may find that starting your own business is the easiest and most profitable source of income. You can also try finding an avenue to work from home (online jobs).

Our Chat with a Local: La Paz

We spoke with La Paz local, Janice, who was originally from Canada. She was walking her little dog on El Malecón when we stopped and spoke with her.

Janice: I'm originally from Ontario, Canada, but I hate the cold. My husband and I were both looking for a warmer climate. We got lucky because a job basically fell into his lap. He was a college instructor and he got an offer to come teach down in Baja, so we jumped at the chance.

I wasn't sure I would like La Paz, because the city itself seems rather congested, but as soon as I saw the waterfront I knew that I could be happy here, as long as we lived close to the water. We got a nice rental near the water and now I walk my dog down here every single day. It's done wonders for my stress levels.

My husband teaches during the day and I work online, but only part-time. We are living comfortably here on a third of what we were earning in Canada. And no more snow!

Cabo San Lucas: Tourism and Nightlife

Why choose Cabo San Lucas?

"Los Cabos" refers to the region that includes Cabo San Lucas, the neighboring city of San José del Cabo, and the 20 or so miles between the two cities. Most of the tourist attractions, such as hotels, beaches, and golf courses, can be found in-between the two cities. This area is commonly referred to as "The Corridor" or "Golden Corridor".

The "Cabo Corridor" between both cities, marking the space between San Jose del Cabo and Cabo San Lucas.

Cabo San Lucas is well-known as an international party hub and vacation spot for tourists and spring breakers looking to enjoy the city's many beautiful beaches, surfing, fishing, and amazing food. But is it a place you can see yourself (and your family) living long-term? There are distinct pros and cons to living in Los Cabos you need to take into account.

Mexico is a popular place to live for retired expats, but many working professionals and families are deciding to give up an often overwhelming, overpriced life in the US and Canada for a fresh start in Mexico. Cabo San Lucas and the entire Los Cabos area in general is becoming one of the most popular regions in Baja California Sur for expats to settle.

There are many activities for tourists and residents to enjoy, the housing and general cost of living is lower, and the area provides great healthcare and educational opportunities for its residents. It's also full of native English speakers, and the possibility that you will be able to communicate in English to anyone in the area is very likely.

While Los Cabos is definitely one of the most "touristy" places in Baja, this region has a lot to offer for expats who don't mind living with a bit of a crowd.

Location, Population, and Size

Cabo San Lucas is located at the southern tip of Mexico's Baja California Sur peninsula.

There are around 68,000 permanent residents living in Cabo San Lucas, plus thousands of tourists on any given day. The population of Los Cabos is predicted to triple in the next two decades, given the increasing popularity of both Cabo San Lucas and San José del Cabo.

The Marina in downtown Cabo San Lucas

The marina has 380 slips with space for yachts and boats up to 200 feet. There is a downtown area surrounding the marina with stores, restaurants, bars, and shops. The very popular Médano beach is within walking distance from downtown Cabo.

This beach is always full of tourists and people trying to sell tours, souvenirs, or timeshares. If you are looking for a quieter beach where locals hang out, try out Cannery beaches or the serene waters of Lover's Beach (*Playa de los Amantes*) which is located next to The Arc, but on the Pacific Ocean side.

"El Arco" or "The Arc", one of the most famous landmarks in Cabo

You can hire a boat to take you there and spend the day exploring the beach, and if the sea level is low, you can even walk under The Arc. Ask the captain to pick you up in the afternoon, or if you don't want to wait for the captain, you can just wave your hand to any of the small boats that take tours to The Arc or Lover's Beach and they can take you back to the Marina.

Be wary of scammers if you do this; some people may offer you a tour to The Arc and they'll have a card hanging from their neck, but that is not an official license. They will charge you double the price you would pay a real captain.

Spotting a Scammer

We had an experience with one of these scammers, who charged 300 pesos. When we asked him where his boat was, he responded, "Don't worry, I am going to get it for you."

The scammer waved his hand and whistled to one captain, who ignored him. After three attempts, one captain sailed to the dock and asked him what he needed. He responded, "These people want to go to The Arc. How much do you charge?" The captain asked him, "How much did *you* charge him?" The guy didn't want to say it in front of us. He said it quietly, but we still heard it. He said 300 pesos. The captain responded, "You are crazy. I don't have time to take him. Besides, you don't even pay your taxes and you just want to make money out of us!"

The captain told us, "If you want to go to The Arc, just go directly to the captain of one of these boats. This guy wants to charge you way more than we would charge you."

Finally, we got lucky and found a boat captain to take us to the arc. They charged 200 pesos (currently about $10-$15 US dollars) for the full tour of the arc without a hassle.

This is just one example of how people might try to scam you if you're not careful. If you want to take a day cruise that can take you to all the different beaches in Los Cabos, it would cost you around $140 US dollars. The tour companies will take you snorkeling and to visit the Arc also. If you find somebody trying to charge you significantly more than that, odds are good you're dealing with a con artist.

The Desert Park Natural Reserve

The Desert Park Natural Reserve is located between Cabo San Lucas and San José del Cabo in the Corridor area. The reserve features mountains, large expanses of desert where visitors can view large cactus and desert animals, and amazing sea views. Visitors can also take camel rides along the beach (yes, that's right—camels, not horses, although there are places where you can rent horses, as well). To appreciate the reserve properly, we recommend taking a guided tour where a local can tell you about the history of the area.

Cabo San Lucas: The Pros

You will never be bored in Cabo San Lucas. There are plenty of activities, both on land and underwater, for people to enjoy. Tours of the local parks and reserves are perfect for nature enthusiasts. You can take your family snorkeling, jet-skiing, banana-boating, or parasailing. If you love fishing, sport fishing is a major industry in Los Cabos.

The many restaurants and bars are perfect for going on a date or enjoying a nice meal with your family. If you enjoy partying, there are a number of bars, pubs, and clubs for you to spend a night out on the town. In fact, Cabo San Lucas is famous for its active nightlife. It attracts a considerable spring break crowd with its reputation for quirky excitement and abandon.

Cabo San Lucas also offers a range of residential property, from the more expensive beachfront properties and gated communities to the more moderate single-family homes. You can live comfortably with all the modern amenities for a fraction of what you would pay in the United States or Canada.

You may find it easy to get around Cabo San Lucas even if you are not fluent in Spanish; however, it's still advisable that you know at least some Spanish before you decide to rent or buy property in any area of Mexico.

Cabo San Lucas: Cons

Cabo Sab Lucas is a popular spot for tourists and spring-breakers, and the city is known for its rowdy nightlife. If you're looking for a quieter city that doesn't cater to tourists, Cabo San Lucas may not be for you. You might want to set your sights on San José del Cabo or Los Barriles to the east instead.

Merchants and the occasional scam artist are on every corner, looking to make some money off the tourists. This kind of crowd can be overwhelming for some people. Note that this is not unique to Mexico and especially not to Los Cabos at large. Pushy vendors can be found in every city that attracts a large number of tourists, but it's especially prevalent in Cabo San Lucas. As always, be vigilant when traveling or moving to a new area and use common sense when meeting strangers.

Cabo San Lucas is in a constant state of change. Previously untouched areas are being bought up by developers to build more golf courses and luxury hotels. Traffic can be a nightmare in denser areas of the city and side streets are always jam-packed with vendors and tourists. If you came to Mexico to get away from the crowds, you'll find this city to be something of a disappointment.

The Weather: Pros

Cabo San Lucas enjoys about 340 days of sunshine with the yearly average temperature sitting at 81°F. The winter months (January through March) are mild and sunny with temperatures ranging from 75°F during the day and 55°F at night. The spring months, which are April through June, average temperatures range from 60 °F at night to 85°F during the day.

July through September are the hottest months of the year with temperatures reaching 75°F during the night and up to 100°F during the day. The late summer months bring the most rain. The fall comes suddenly in October with average temperatures ranging from 63 °F during the night and 85°F during the day.

Sea temperatures vary, but the average temperature is around 70°F. However, if you plan to go swimming or surfing, do make sure the beach is swimmable. The tides are safer here than the ones in nearby San José del Cabo, but some of the beaches are too dangerous for swimming. Always double-check before you enter the water.

The Weather: Cons

If you don't enjoy living in a hot climate, Cabo San Lucas will be an awfully hard sell. Although temperatures are comfortable for most of the year, summer temperatures can reach up into the triple-digits. Temperatures do not reach freezing by the coast, but can drop below freezing inland and on the nearby Laguna Mountains. The appeal of living in a tropical area is consistently warm weather, but Cabo San Lucas does see erratic temperature changes from time to time.

The rainy season runs from June to October, with the bulk of the rainfall in August and September. During these months, you can expect heavy rain several times a week. Tropical storms and the occasional hurricane may also land in Cabo San Lucas in August or September. These storms can bring violent winds, heavy rain, and flooding. Hurricanes usually don't make landfall, but when they do, they tend to do a lot of damage.

A few years ago, Hurricane Odile hit an unprepared Cabo San Lucas and caused major damage to the city's hotels, shops, and infrastructure. Over 90% of Baja California Sur's population was left without power. Fortunately, Cabo San Lucas quickly bounced back. More recently, Hurricane Newton hit Cabo San Lucas and caused flooding and a few trees to fall down throughout the city. The most damage occurred along beachfront property. You'll be safe in Cabo San Lucas as long as you pay attention to hurricane warnings, but there's always the risk of seeing your property damaged or even destroyed by these natural disasters.

Local Population: Pros

One of the major advantages of living in a resort town is how much easier it is to integrate. Because so many people from other countries visit or move here, Cabo San Lucas is a fairly inclusive city. Most of the expats you meet here will have migrated from the United States. In fact, about 80 percent of people originating from the United States who live in Baja California choose to live in Los Cabos.

The major advantage is that the language and social barriers that come from moving to another country are not difficult to breach. It's easy to find people who speak English in Cabo San Lucas. There are several newsletters published in English that cover news specifically for expats in the Cabo area.

Having a large crowd of foreigners living here means you'll be surrounded by a fairly diverse crowd consisting of Mexican-born citizens, expats from foreign countries, and tourists from around the world. This diversity helps make it easier to become part of the crowd.

In smaller towns, an expat might stand out and struggle to integrate, but here, you can melt right in, even if you don't speak Spanish. Communities within communities of expats will serve as a helpful "safety net" to help you adjust and find your place here. The city has seen rapid growth over the years, which means there will be plenty of room for you to move in and become a part of the city.

Local Population: Cons

Of all the places in Baja California Sur, Cabo San Lucas is definitely one of the most wild. With its rowdy nightclub scene and reputation as the main hub of partying and entertainment, it's no wonder this city has become such a popular destination for tourists and spring break partygoers.

Cabo San Lucas is a great destination if you're looking for fun and excitement as a tourist. As an expat, however, the energy and quirky chaos, especially from the nightlife, can be exhausting to live around. Life in Cabo San Lucas has its quieter moments too, but the main draw of this city is partying. If you're looking for peace and quiet, you won't find it here (but you will find it in San José del Cabo, which we will discuss later).

Because of its reputation as a party central, Cabo San Lucas is positively swarming with tourists. If you live near the nightclubs, you may have to deal with people wandering around who have had too much to drink, so it pays to be extra cautious when driving at night. You also won't get very much of the authentic Baja experience here. If you're looking for culture, you might have better luck in San José del Cabo, Cabo San Lucas' more reserved sister city.

Some local shops in downtown Cabo San Lucas, near the Marina

To put it bluntly, if you don't want to live where there are tons of tourists partying late at night, you don't want to live here.

If you don't mind a very active nightlife scene, or if you want to start a business like a bar or a restaurant, you'll get on just fine in Cabo San Lucas. It all depends on how much tolerance you have for the resort scene. There is certainly money to be made here if you speak English and want to cater to American and Canadian tourists.

Cost of Housing: Pros

Ocean-front or ocean-view property in the United States, Canada, or Europe is often simply too expensive for most people. As a result of these sky-high costs, potential homebuyers are looking to Mexico for similar homes with less frightening price tags. Housing prices in Los Cabos have increased in the last decade due to increased development and demand from foreign buyers.

However, you can still get a moderately-sized single-family home near the ocean for a reasonable price. Beachfront properties will cost considerably more than property further inland, but compared to beachfront property costs in other countries, it's a bargain.

Mexico is also attractive to potential buyers because it offers a range of residential properties. There are gated communities full of single-family homes, beachfront condos, and beautiful villas along the beach. You can also find homes further inland. These properties are usually less expensive than the ones along the water. If you are only looking to live in Cabo San Lucas for a few months out of the year, there are a number of timeshare houses in and around Los Cabos.

Timeshares in general are a very popular business, though you do need to watch out for con artists and timeshare scams, which are common. If in doubt, avoid buying from anyone but developers or licensed real estate agents, like Remax Mexico. Listings can be found online or in newspaper advertisements. Before taking a leap and purchasing property, it's imperative to actually visit Cabo San Lucas to get an idea of actual costs and see which neighborhoods you prefer.

For those only looking to rent property in Cabo San Lucas, most rental properties are offered through local realty agents or by individual property owners. These properties can also be found online or in newspapers, but it may help to walk around Cabo San Lucas, as there are often ads for rental properties in front of local restaurants and shops. If you are interested in renovating an old home or buying a lot and building your own home, consider eco-housing.

We've all heard about reducing one's carbon footprint. Renovating or building a home in Mexico's natural environment gives you the opportunity to live in an energy-efficient home that helps benefit the planet and give you a comfortable place to live. Rooftop solar panels are common in Baja, as are solar water heaters. They save electricity (which tends to be expensive in Mexico) and are an effective way to power your home in an area that gets a lot of sunlight all year long.

Cost of Housing: Cons

The increase in development and expats choosing the live in Cabo San Lucas has led to a rise in housing prices over the last two decades. If you know you want to buy or rent property in Cabo San Lucas, there is no time like the present. There's no telling what prices will look like in the future. Wait too long, and you could miss a prime deal.

Make sure that all of your paperwork is in order to rent or buy property. This includes visas, lending documents, and your housing contract (or lease agreement, if renting). Always use a trusted source when buying a home. Take the time to ask other expats how they went about renting or buying property.

Healthcare

Healthcare costs in Mexico vary based on the city, hospital, and the patient's health concerns. The quality of healthcare coverage also varies depending on your location. You should research the hospitals and medical offices located in the area you are interested in moving to. Overall, health care costs, including medical insurance, surgery, prescription drugs and routine medical care are much cheaper in Mexico versus the US. Many expats visit Mexico specifically for this purpose.

Over 50 million people receive coverage through Mexico's state sponsored healthcare provider, *Instituto Mexicano del Seguro Social* (IMSS). IMSS provides affordable health insurance for all residents regardless of their nationality.

You can also find quality healthcare services offered through private clinics. These outpatient clinics are ideal for non-life-threatening medical issues like sprains and broken bones.

The cost of healthcare in Mexico can be considerably lower than in the United States. Of course, it depends on the doctor, but prescription drugs, lab tests, overnight stays in a private hospital room, and even a trip to the dentist will typically be less expensive in Mexico.

There are several hospitals in Mexico and there is at least one top-notch hospital located in every mid-sized-to-large metropolitan area. Cabo San Lucas has two major hospitals: *Amerimed American Hospital,* which is located in the center of the city, and *Blue Medical Net*, which is located in between Cabo San Lucas and San José del Cabo.

Employment for Expats: Pros

With a city this bustling and full of tourist activity, there's plenty of work to be found. You'll have several options for employment. Real estate is one of the bigger contenders out there, which is no surprise, given the growth this city has seen in such a short span of time. Many expats come down to the area and become real estate agents or loan officers catering specifically to the large American and Canadian expat community.

Of course, you can also work online or even start your own business, but perhaps the easiest work to get is at the resorts. Because tourism is such a profitable industry in Los Cabos, resorts and other tourism businesses are always searching for fluent English-speakers. If you're interested at all in working with tourists, Cabo San Lucas is possibly the best place in Baja California Sur to look for a job.

Employment for Expats: Cons

Getting a job in Mexico is generally tricky, because you need residency to get a job. A visitor's visa will not allow you to work legally in the country. Of course, if you work online, that's not a problem, but if you want to work for a resort or open a business in Mexico, then you will need to apply for residency.

It's the proverbial carrot being held over your head, and it can be maddening. Make sure you have all your paperwork in order and be prepared to go through some hoops in order to obtain residency. That will make the transition process much easier in the long run.

Our Chat with a Local: Cabo San Lucas

We chatted with Reggie, a Cabo San Lucas resident who specializes in selling insurance to Americans and Canadian expats

Reggie: I'm originally from Orange County, California. Orange County is a very affluent area in Southern California. We liked it there, but it was so expensive. The cost of living is insane, and it only seemed to get worse as we got older. And the traffic became intolerable, too. We decided to make a change.

My wife and I sold our home during the housing boom in 2003. Instead of buying another expensive home in

California, we took our profits and moved down to Cabo San Lucas. There was plenty of opportunity for us here. We didn't do anything in a rush—we saved our money and planned every decision very carefully.

We used a local attorney to get Mexican Residency. What we had in the bank was plenty in order to prove we could support ourselves. We rented for a few years and finally decided to buy property when we found something we really liked.

Cabo has a lot of business opportunities for Americans who want to cater to expats and tourists. I sell all types of insurance, including health insurance and auto insurance. Most of my clients are expats from the US who live in Los Cabos most of the year.

My wife and I ended up purchasing the building where my office is located and now we have rental income from the businesses that are here. Since we're here all day running our own business anyway, we can keep an eye on the place. There's plenty of opportunity here if you want it.

San José del Cabo: The Calmer Side of Cabo

Los Cabos is an undeniable hotspot for tourist activity in Baja California Sur. San José del Cabo and its nearby neighboring city, Cabo San Lucas, are similar to each other in many ways, but there are certain distinctions that help San José del Cabo stand out as its own, unique city. If you want to expatriate to Cabo, you will need to do your research to decide which of the "Los Cabos" cities is the best place for you.

Cabo San Lucas has something of a reputation for its party scene, being a prime destination for spring break and other kinds of exciting, raucous events.

San José del Cabo, on the other hand, is a little quieter, a little slower, and a bit less focused on partying. This is of great appeal especially to expats who would like to move here and start a new life. While tourists flock to both cities, San José del Cabo is just a little bit more geared toward everyday living, rather than nonstop play. If you want to raise a family in Baja, then San José del Cabo is somewhat more suited for that. Paired with the many excellent bilingual schools in the area, this is a good place to raise children if you're really looking to make your life in Baja California Sur as a Mexican resident or Mexican citizen.

The high concentration of expats already living here also means you will have a fairly large network of people to communicate with and get advice from on how to adjust to the move. Cabo San Lucas has this too, but San José del Cabo has the slight advantage of its reputation for being not being quite as wild, attracting a less party-oriented crowd looking to expatriate. If a more relaxed pace is what you're looking for, you will find many other like-minded people here.

A view from the Cabo Corridor; the beachfront homes have breathtaking views

Even though San José del Cabo has a reputation of being more laid-back (locals refer to it as a "sleepy" resort town), this city has plenty of interesting activities you can participate in to pass the time. Cabo Pulmo Marine Park is one of the most popular tourist destinations outside of the resort hotels. Here, you can participate in a many different watersports, like kayaking or snorkeling.

The main attraction of Cabo Pulmo Marine Park, though, is getting to see the wildlife. The coral reefs are beautiful to behold and many people like to visit in order to spot sea lions, whales, and turtles. Many rare and endangered animals live here, so if you are a nature enthusiast, you will want to visit this park and spend some time admiring the wildlife here.

One thing you'll notice is that San José del Cabo is very welcoming toward visitors, whether they are just staying for a vacation or permanently immigrating. There are a lot of expats living in this city, mostly from the United States. There is also a sizable population of Canadian expats living in San José del Cabo. You can expect to fit in with the community with relative ease thanks to the high saturation of expats already living among the locals. It's a good place to settle for retirees, as well.

San José del Cabo may be a resort town, but there's more to see here than just the beaches. If you're more interested in the culture of Baja, you won't be disappointed. Although not considered as "authentic" as what you might experience in some smaller towns, this city does pay homage to its cultural roots and celebrate its history. San José del Cabo, like many other cities and towns in Baja California Sur, has an annual festival to celebrate the city's patron saint.

The *Fiesta de San José* is an 11-day festival that takes place in the month of March. It is one of the major events here and includes a large variety of traditional festivities. The *fiesta* kicks off on the evening of March 8 with music and parties. During the weekend, the locals will hold parades and carnivals where you can find food vendors selling traditional cuisine, such as tamales and sugared pumpkin candies. If you want to immerse yourself in the local culture, then you absolutely don't want to miss this festival—but with 11 days of celebration, you can hardly miss it.

Also of note in this city is the beautiful 18th century architecture, parts of the city's history since its colonization by the Spanish in 1730. The locals have taken great care in preserving these old buildings and monuments for posterity.

You can find old missions and other pieces of history here, and all of these old buildings have stories behind them. Between the traditional festival in March, preserved historical sites, and careful conservation of the wildlife in the marine park, this city has a certain old-world beauty and genuineness that Cabo San Lucas falls a bit short of, as many people who have moved here can attest to.

The entire Los Cabos region has a reputation as a tourism dynamo for a reason, but even though these two cities have a lot in common, you will find many subtle differences between them. If you want to have some fun and excitement in your new home, Cabo San Lucas will definitely do the trick. But if you're looking for something a little more laid-back while still having that sense of fun and energy in the background, you'll be very happy living in San José del Cabo.

Location, Population, and Size

San José del Cabo is only a short drive away from its neighboring city, Cabo San Lucas. Collectively, these two cities are referred to as Los Cabos or sometimes just "Cabo". Their general location, climate, population, and geography are similar, though not completely identical.

San José del Cabo is the seat of Los Cabos municipality and one of the larger cities in Baja. Its popularity as both a tourist destination and as a place for expats to settle down has steadily increased its population over the years. The population of permanent residents is about 70,000 people. However, tourists swell these numbers dramatically. Between this city and the neighboring Cabo San Lucas, the amount of visitors staying in the area has reached over 900,000 (almost 1 million people!) during especially busy years. The difference is that the tourists are just transient visitors, and they go home once the busy season is over.

Like its neighboring cities, San José del Cabo is situated on the Tropic of Cancer at the southernmost tip of Baja California Sur. To be precise, it is located right at the end of the cape (or *cabo*, which is where the name "Los Cabos" comes from). San José del Cabo has slightly warmer weather than Cabo San Lucas overall. While people admire the beaches of Los Cabos, the shores around this city have dangerous riptides, and many tourists have drowned because they did not heed posted warning signs.

Beaches of San José del Cabo

Most beaches in San José del Cabo are generally **unsafe for swimming**, so always check before you go into the water. That being said, even the beaches unsuitable for swimming still have remarkable views and the sunrise in San José del Cabo is worth getting up early to see.

Some of the best beaches are found along the marina, such as *La Playita*. If you want to go swimming, you're much better off taking a visit to the considerably safer beaches in Cabo San Lucas, but if you want to just relax and enjoy the tropical weather, any of the beaches in San José del Cabo will do. In addition, the fishing is very robust. In fact, fishing is actually a big part of the economy. You can spend hours just reeling in the catch of the day from a boat or from the shore. Just be sure conditions are safe first before you go out on a boat, particularly during the hottest months of the year (especially September), when hurricanes are known to form.

*Beautiful Palmilla Beach with its pristine blue waters,
perfect for swimming*

For those who want to live in Baja California Sur to enjoy the tropical waves, knowing the beaches are unsafe for swimming can seem like a huge deal-breaker. However, if you want to live in this city and still enjoy the ocean, there are many nearby beaches that are fairly safe as long as you check the conditions before entering the water.

Some of these "safe" beaches include: *La Playita* outside of San José, Palmilla, Chileno, Santa Maria, and Barco Varado in the Corridor, and Médano and *Playa del Amor* in Cabo San Lucas. Most of the swimmable beaches are outside the actual city of San José del Cabo, but they're all a fairly short distance away (less than 10 minutes by car).

Dangerous Riptides in Los Cabos

The riptides are a major hazard here. Many people have drowned because of dangerous riptides that can easily catch an unsuspecting swimmer or surfer by surprise. Take any warning of dangerous tides seriously, and if you have children with you, make sure they stay away from the ocean unless the beach has lifeguards and is specifically safe to swim. A visibly calm ocean does not mean that the water is safe to swim. Dangerous undertows can occur on ocean beaches that look safe to an outside observer. For your personal reference, we have listed some of the safest beaches in the city.

Even at these locations, however, we advise you to be cautious. Avoid entering the water altogether unless a lifeguard is present.

Chileno Beach and Chileno Bay

This beautiful beach is one of the swimmable beaches you can find in the Cabo Corridor. It is located about 15 minutes from San José del Cabo and Cabo San Lucas. Chileno bay is well-known for its coral. Schools of fish can also be found in these waters.

Santa Maria Beach

Santa Maria Beach is another safe beach for swimming located in the Cabo Corridor, two minutes from Chileno Bay. This beach and Chileno have *palapas* (A palapa is an open dwelling with a thatched roof made of dried palm leaves) where you can relax. Just try to get up early so you can get your spot.

A simple beach palapa

This beach also includes a *palapa* for handicapped people with a flat ramp for access by wheelchair (handicapped accommodations can be rare in Mexico, since the laws for accessibility are different there), which you can reach by following the asphalt pathway that goes from the parking lot to the beach. Tours from Cabo San Lucas come to this beach to see the teeming schools of fish that populate this part of the bay.

Playa Acapulquito and Palmilla Beach

Playa Acapulquito is a nice swimmable beach. It's a little bit tricky to reach this area, because you have to pass under a tunnel, and to get to the tunnel, you have to go down some stairs. It is not a good beach for handicapped people, because there is no easy access to the beach if you can't walk.

It is located next to the 7 Seas Hotel and Restaurant, which is about five minutes outside central San José del Cabo. Playa Acapulquito is about two minutes away from Palmilla beach.

Because Palmilla is easier to reach and has more parking spaces, it's often more crowded than Acapulquito beach.

Palmilla Beach Area

Palmilla beach is one of the most popular beaches in San José del Cabo. This beach is safe for swimmers. Its easy access and plentiful parking space makes it one of the most visited beaches in San José. Palmilla is one of the most beautiful and exclusive places in Los Cabos to live.

Some of the homes cost millions of dollars, and there is a golf course that regularly attracts the rich and famous. The beach is open to everyone, however.

Palmilla Beach small, beautiful is located about seven minutes (by car) from San José del Cabo.

Another shot of the gorgeous Palmilla Beach area. Our pictures do not do it justice. The snorkeling here was incredible.

In Palmilla beach, there is a lifeguard on duty, just as there is in Chileno and Santa Maria. What makes Palmilla special is its superior accommodation for visitors in wheelchairs. The lifeguard uses a little *carrito* (a special wheeled chair with thick tires that can move in sandy terrain) to take wheelchair-bound visitors to the beach so they can enjoy the waves.

Las Viudas Beach

This beach, located in the Cabo Corridor, is better admired from the shore. The tides are not as dangerous, but we still don't recommend trying to swim here. Instead, it's the view that makes this place noteworthy. However, the shore does have some beautiful scenery. This is a great place to relax and just listen to the waves breaking on the rocks.

San José del Cabo: The Pros

This city is sometimes described as being a "calmer" version of the wilder Cabo San Lucas. There's a bit less tourist action here.

Although it's still a tourist hotspot, there's a very easy-going vibe here. As tourist zones go, it's a mostly-relaxed atmosphere. Combined with the pleasant tropical weather, it's no wonder that San José del Cabo has become a popular spot for expats and tourists alike.

San José del Cabo: Cons

Even though it's not quite as wild as Cabo San Lucas, make no mistake, this is very much a tourist city. This means that there are tourist dollars here, if you're looking to start a business catering specifically to tourists.

If you're looking to retire or someplace quiet and out-of-the-way, there are certainly parts of the city that offer quiet areas away from the usual bustle. Even if you choose to live in a quieter part of the city, though, you really won't be able to get away from the fact that tourists are always present throughout Los Cabos.

If you are particularly averse to the idea of being surrounded by tourism, you may want to think twice about moving here, (or anywhere in Los Cabos, for that matter).

Although the beaches in San José del Cabo are spectacular, they are generally not safe to swim in due to dangerous riptides (with the exception of a handful of "safe" beaches).

That in itself can be a huge disappointment, since Los Cabos is known for its beautiful beaches and ocean views. If you plan on spending a lot of time swimming or surfing, you will need to take the time to find out where the few swimmable beaches are. Otherwise, you will have to commute a little out of your way to one of the beaches in Cabo San Lucas instead.

What Makes San José del Cabo Unique?

San José del Cabo and Cabo San Lucas tend to be lumped together as a single place. It can be easy to confuse these two resort cities, but they are not the same!

Residents of San José del Cabo will tell you that their city is far less geared toward catering to tourists. It tends to keep the bulk of its tourist activity isolated to the resorts while regular residents enjoy a quieter life.

One thing the residents are proud of is the city's historic architecture, some of which dates back to colonial times. Two of the more notable buildings are the *Misión de San José del Cabo Anuiti* and City Hall. The city hall building celebrates the local history with a mural depicting scenes of everyday life in Baja throughout its past. The city also features a number of art galleries, particularly downtown. Every Thursday during July through November, the city hosts an art walk where visitors and residents alike can visit these galleries and admire the works of local artists and see new exhibitions.

Locals of San José del Cabo refer to their city as having an air of sophistication. Fine wine, fine dining, and upscale shopping are all parts of the city's culture.

You can purchase high-quality artisan goods at the *Plaza Artesanos*, which is right next to the historic district. Salsa-dancing and beer-tasting at the local microbrewery are two of the more popular activities.

San José del Cabo also has an active but restrained nightlife. There are several nightclubs and bars to choose from. For those seeking more exciting pursuits, there's the *Canopy Costa Azul Xtreme*, a thrilling zip line tour over the canyons, giving you the most spectacular natural views on a high-adrenaline ride. If you want to slow down and take in the sights up-close, you can also visit *Estero San José*, which is a great place to admire the local flora and do some birdwatching.

For those who want to make a life here, this city's more mellow and reserved attitude makes it more attractive than the rowdier Cabo San Lucas. The two cities that make up Los Cabos are similar in many ways, but if you take the time to talk to people who live here, they'll tell you San José del Cabo is still very much its own city with its own atmosphere and unique way of life.

The Weather: Pros

San José del Cabo enjoys the same pleasantly warm tropical climate that most of the Baja California Sur region experiences. Despite its close proximity to Cabo San Lucas, this city is actually a little bit warmer than its southwestern neighbor.

Whether this is a pro or not greatly depends on what kind of weather you like, but if you do prefer the weather to be warm-to-hot all year, you'll find that here. The city, like most tropical cities, is warm year-round and while the temperature can soar to the double-digits during just about any month. The daily average temperature usually ranges from the high sixties to the low eighties.

If you don't care for cold weather or rain, you'll be pleased to know that rainfall is infrequent here. The driest season is spring, but even during the months with the most amount of rain, you can expect to see only a handful of rainy days. Don't expect just a light drizzle on those days, though. When it *does* rain, it tends to be quite a downpour and flooding can happen, but during most of the year, there's very little precipitation.

The temperature of the sea ranges from the low seventies in the coldest months to the low eighties in the warmest, so as long as you are at a beach with safe tides, you'll find the water very pleasant to swim and surf in no matter what time of year it is. If you're interested in surfing, you'll find the breaks during the spring and summer months are better in the east. During the fall and winter, however, the surfing is better around the West Cape. Regardless of the season, make sure the beach is safe for surfing first.

The Weather: Cons

Weather in this city is somewhat erratic and hard to predict, though you can expect the average day to be hot and dry. Like most of the peninsula, it has a generally arid climate, but it's not unheard-of for the area to see spates of heavy rainfall brought in by tropical cyclones from the south.

On the other hand, it's just as likely you will see almost no rain at all for extended periods of time. If there is any rain during any given year, you can expect to see most of it in September, which is usually the rainiest month in Los Cabos. It's also the month most likely to see a hurricane, though hurricane season itself actually extends from June to October, which also happen to be the hottest months of the year.

The hurricanes don't always reach land, but when they do, it's usually between August or September, when the temperature of the ocean rises. The damage from hurricanes that reach land can be extensive, so always pay close attention to the warnings and remember that when it comes to hurricanes, being overly-cautious is a safer bet than not being cautious enough.

Local Population: Pros

Perhaps the biggest advantage to living in a city famous for its tourist attractions is the relative ease of moving in as an expat. Moving to a new country is always going to result in some level of culture shock, but the transition is a little more forgiving when you're surrounded with other people who are also from outside of Mexico.

Furthermore, this place is a lightning rod for expats and retirees from the United States, Canada, and Europe. You will find it easy to meet other people who know all about the expat life. You'll also find many people here who speak English, which is very helpful if your Spanish is a bit rusty.

Local Population: Cons

It goes without saying at this point, but if you do not want to be surrounded by tourists, you are not going to be happy living here. The entire region is famous for its tourism industry and you will be seeing a lot of visitors to this city throughout the year. There are certainly parts of the city that are less saturated with tourists, but it's still part of the lifestyle and fabric of San José del Cabo. The same is true for its neighboring city, Cabo San Lucas.

You can expect that this place will feel a bit crowded, especially on weekends and holidays. Although San José del Cabo isn't as big as Cabo San Lucas, the dense crowds of visitors, incoming expats, and retirees throughout the year build into a pretty heavy crowd, especially in the downtown areas and beaches.

Cost of Housing: Pros

Being a sizable city, San José del Cabo has plenty of residential housing. If you're looking for a place to live, you can easily find a nice house for sale for just under $100,000 USD, which is a pretty good bargain anywhere this close to a lovely beach.

You can also find condos, long-term rentals, and undeveloped lots waiting for your custom home plans. A quick search online for housing in San José del Cabo yields significant results, so you'll have plenty of options to choose from. Just be sure that you are up-to-date on how owning property works for foreigners. While almost anyone can purchase property in Mexico, it will be easier for you to do the paperwork once you have permanent residency status in Mexico.

The cost of living in general is fairly reasonable in San José del Cabo, as it is in most of Baja. This is especially true when compared to popular coastal cities in the US or Canada. Baja is much cheaper comparatively.

Combined with the low housing costs, it's reasonably inexpensive to live comfortably (despite it being a resort city). Although the cost of living is low, you can find almost any convenience you're looking for here, from essentials like excellent medical care to lifestyle activities like gym memberships. Costco, Wal-Mart, and Home Depot are all within 15 minutes of San José del Cabo, so you will have almost all the modern amenities that you are accustomed to.

Cost of Housing: Cons
Money-wise, there aren't really any major downsides to the cost of housing in this city. Compared to other places in Baja California Sur, the cost is neither notably high nor low. It's simply average for the area in general. The housing market does have a tendency to fluctuate, so you'll have to account for a bit of unpredictability depending on how the economy is as well as how well the tourist industry is doing in the particular year that you want to purchase or rent.

If you're looking to move here for the cheaper cost compared to where you live now, you most likely won't be disappointed. The cost of living in most parts of Mexico is low on the International Cost of Living Index. Baja California Sur is no exception.

That being said, while the price is right, you do need to understand how property ownership works in Mexico. Unless you get legal residency in Mexico, you may not be able to own property outright.

Employment for Expats: Pros

Because this city is so heavily saturated by expats, it will be much easier for you to find a place to work and become part of the community. You can make connections with other expats here and form business networks more easily than you would in a city or town that has very few expats.

There is a great deal of diversity in the kinds of expats you will meet here. Not only will you find people from a wide range of countries (though most of them are from the United States or Canada), but you'll find people of all ages and interests, from students to retirees. Whatever work you want to get into, you'll find at least a few expats who have made it into the field and can help you figure out how to get there too.

Tourism is the number-one industry of Los Cabos, so there's always work to be found in that field, but even getting away from the resorts, you will find plenty of opportunities for employment.

Beyond the tropical paradise image, San José del Cabo is still a city like most others, with people just going about their daily work. Just about any business you would expect to see in a city in the United States or Canada will also be present here.

There are many businesses that cater specifically to expats. Some examples include: English-speaking day spas, shipping and mailbox services, and tax and accounting services for expats.

Employment for Expats: Cons

A big resort city like San José del Cabo has many job opportunities, especially related to tourism. There is already a large network of expats who have gone through the process of moving here and know what it takes to make a life in this city. The economy in Los Cabos is generally good thanks to the constant flow of money coming in from tourists, so there are certainly many jobs to be found. A quick search on Google can show you a sample of the job listings available—a number of them calling for native English speakers, no less.

That being said, the main disadvantage to getting a job here is more or less the same hurdle you will have to jump anywhere else in Mexico. Getting a job as a foreigner involves dealing with a lot of red tape in the process of procuring permanent residency. Using an attorney can make this job a lot easier, of course, but it's still a process that can take a while.

You cannot get a job in Mexico with just a visitor's visa, nor can you own private property. If you're planning to expatriate here, you need to commit to the move and become a resident before you can start looking to get a job and settling down.

Our Chat with a Local: San Jose Del Cabo

In San Jose del Cabo, we spoke with Henry, who was a retiree and a former Texas resident. He owns a condo on the Cabo Real Golf Course and lives in San Jose Del Cabo for at least 6 months every year.

Henry: My wife and I have always liked San Jose del Cabo much better than Cabo San Lucas. We love to golf, so we settled at the Cabo Real Golf Course, which is near the Hilton Hotel. It's less than a mile away from the beach. We love it here. It's beautiful all year round, and I've always felt safe. We've been coming down here for ten years, and I've never had a single problem.

Now that there's a Costco down here, we can find almost everything that we enjoyed back in the US. Even the furniture and the snacks are the same. I just got a leather recliner last week that's almost identical to the one I had in my TV room in Texas.

We go back and forth a lot, but this year, we'll only be going back to Texas for Christmas. The rest of the year, we'll be staying in Mexico. Funny thing is, when I go back to Texas, my buddies ask me about crime, and I tell them, "there is no crime"—at least that I can see. I've never had anything stolen, never been mugged, nothing.

There were over 300 murders in Houston just last year! But my friends back in Texas feel safe, even though the crime in their own hometown in staggering.

I think people just have a mixed-up impression of how violent Mexico is—of course there are bad areas, (just like there are bad areas in the US, too—I wouldn't ever want to live in Chicago [laughter]) but Los Cabos is incredibly safe to live. And also so beautiful!

Where else in the world can you golf all day long surrounded by palm trees and a beautiful ocean less than a 10 minute walk away for this price?

Todos Santos: Artsy and Artisanal

Are you a hobbyist interested in finding a place among nature that's a little more remote than the typical tourist destinations of Los Cabos? Do you love the ocean and dream of surfing on the waves of the tropical Pacific? Do you want to settle down among a lively community of artists and artisans? If you answered yes to any of these, Todos Santos might just be the place for you.

Unlike the more metropolitan areas surrounding it, Todos Santos is a laid-back and somewhat out-of-the-way town with a mellow but welcoming attitude. While tourists flock to bigger, flashier cities like Cabo San Lucas, Todos Santos is a jewel of a town with a small population and a comparatively obscure status.

Located about an hour away from both La Paz and Cabo San Lucas, it's away from the usual crowds and bustle, yet close enough to the cities that you can easily make your way there to get whatever isn't readily available in the town. It's an ideal balance of feeling remote without all the drawbacks of actually *being* remote.

Todos Santos boasts an interesting and vibrant history. Colonized in 1723, Todos Santos began with the building of missions and went by the full name of *Santa Rosa de Todos Santos*. The newly-settled town was ravaged by an epidemic and nearly abandoned until the

1840s, when it was revived as a sugar cane production center.

Over time, eight sugar mills were built and town began to prosper and grow. By the 19th century, it was a thriving town with a rich art culture, particularly where theater and crafts were concerned. Sugar proved to be a dependable source of income for Todos Santos for nearly a century, until a devastating drought destroyed the sugar cane crop. The town was abandoned once again, until 1881, when the water returned to the mesa and ended the long drought.

The twice-abandoned ghost town slowly came back to life, bringing in new crowds of people looking to settle among the beautiful scenery and beaches. Today, numerous ruins of the town that once was still linger, a testament to Todos Santos' fascinating history.

Todos Santos is well-known for its love of the arts, whether it's a traditional craft or something a little more modern and esoteric. You can expect to see galleries full of the works of local artists and artisans.

All throughout the year, several arts festivals are held by the locals. The most notable of these festivals, the Todos Santos Music Festival, is held every February. This event celebrates theater, dance, music, exhibitions, and culinary arts, among other things. In addition, there is a reggae festival, a Latino film festival, and celebrations in honor of several patron saints. If you have any kind of artistic passion, you can expect it to be represented in Todos Santos.

Handpainted face masks in downtown Todos Santos

Natural splendor abounds in Todos Santos and those who are interested in eco-friendly hobbies will feel right at home here. Hiking, surfing, birdwatching, and kayaking are just a few of the activities available to you. If you're into photography, you'll also find many worthwhile subjects to capture on film, whether it's the sprawling beaches, the local wildlife, the ruins of the missions and sugar mills, or the lively sights of the local culture and festivals. In addition, yoga and martial arts are also popular pastimes, as is fishing.

If you're looking to settle down somewhere slow-paced but with a robust culture, Todos Santos has a lot to offer. The town is presently in the process of growing and developing, making more room for people who want to expatriate and begin a life here.

Location, Population and Size

Todos Santos is near the southernmost regions of Baja California Sur, located on the west coast facing the Pacific Ocean. It's is the second-largest town in the La Paz municipality, nestled in the foothills of the Sierra de la Laguna Mountains, about 40 miles north of Cabo San Lucas and just an hour's drive from La Paz. The town is perched on a mesa about a mile from the Pacific, overlooking a scenic valley of flower gardens.

While the population is fairly small, word has begun to spread about the beauty and peace of Todos Santos, gradually turning it into a more popular destination for visitors and expats. However, it still remains a relatively quiet town without the usual energy and fuss of cities that have a large tourism industry.

Todos Santos: The Pros

The main charm of Todos Santos is its relatively obscure status. With a fairly small population, it's not as overcrowded as some of the more touristy parts of the region. It has many excellent surf spots, a variety of wildlife and lush flora, and pleasant tropical weather throughout most of the year. The many beautiful views in the town make it a prime spot for photography.

Todos Santos also offers something for the history buff. Old missions and ruins of sugar mills left abandoned in the '50s can be found throughout the town, crumbling and overtaken by flowering vines. It's also a great destination for artists. Art in its various mediums, from culinary to choreography, is a big part of the local culture, as are eco-friendly activities. Nature lovers will find plenty to appreciate and even have the opportunity to help care for the wildlife.

Todos Santos: Cons

The town is becoming more well-known for its laid-back and remote atmosphere and has started to attract more tourists and visitors. It still remains a much less hectic destination than some larger cities, but the influx of new residents has changed the atmosphere somewhat. The benefit to this is a greater increase in modern conveniences as the town becomes more developed, but those who came in search of the land's pristine, undeveloped natural beauty may find this off-putting.

In addition to the increase in visitors, Todos Santos is seeing a rise in real estate prices by virtue of demand. If you're planning to move here, buy as soon as possible while the price is as low as it can be, but make sure you don't get taken in by a scam artist. Be timely, but not overly hasty.

The Weather: Pros

Todos Santos has an interesting mix of arid mesa and tropical shores, contrasting scenery of cacti and dry shrubs cast against the horizon of the Pacific. The area enjoys pleasantly moderate tropical weather throughout most of the year. The average temperature is around 77 degrees Fahrenheit, dropping to the mid-50s to 60s during the evening. You can expect to feel the cooling Pacific breeze during most of the day, which keeps the weather nice and balmy even during the summer, when other parts of Baja California Sur start to get hot. The hottest parts of the year are August and September, but you can expect the weather to stay below triple digits even during the peak of the season. The beaches also provide excellent surfing spots throughout the year.

A downtown surf shop in Todos Santos

The Weather: Cons

For the most part, the weather is Todos Santos is very pleasant, but it does have its share of storms. The biggest danger is hurricanes. You'll want to pay close attention to any weather warnings you see, and you might find yourself losing power during a particularly nasty storm. Less hazardous than hurricanes but still a serious matter are the tropical storms, which bring with them heavy rain and lightning.

As with many parts of the Baja California Sur coast, you must be careful about which beaches you choose to surf or swim at. There are only a few beaches that are safe for swimming in Todos Santos. In particular, be wary of the *Las Pocitas* beach to the north of the town. Although it's a lovely area, there's an occasional undertow during big swells. *Playa Las Cerritos* is a much safer beach for swimmers, and is also an excellent place for collecting seashells.

Local Population: Pros

If you're looking for a place that isn't overrun with tourists, this is the spot for you. The small population means less of a crowd to deal with and more space for you to enjoy the tropical weather and natural surroundings. Even though it's becoming a more popular visiting destination for eco-tourists and other expats, you'll find it's not nearly as congested as most of the cities.

If you're especially interested in the arts, you'll find this place a good fit for you. The springtime is filled with festivals and other events. Arts, crafts, and other types of artisanal work are a common sight. You can sample food from local vendors, such as traditionally-prepared tamales.

Aside from the arts, you'll also find a huge variety of recreational activities, including surfing, fishing, hiking, kayaking, and yoga. Many people living in the area have a great deal of interest in the environment. Bird watching, whale watching, and turtle nest protection are all common activities. Many of the tourists who visit go on eco-tours, enjoying the sights of the natural world in the tropical paradise.

Local Population: Cons

Expect to see a lot of surfers, fishers, artists, and New Age-type people living alongside the locals. If you find yourself comfortable in these crowds, you'll fit in just fine, but if none of these groups match your lifestyle or interests, you may be better off someplace else. With such a small population, life can get lonely if you find yourself the outlier in the crowd.

It is also worth noting that while the major charm of Todos Santos is the comparatively fewer tourists, expect to see a lot of eco-tourists and surfers among the visitors who do come. If your goal is to find a place with absolutely no tourism, unfortunately, Todos Santos will not meet your goals and it is likely to see an increase in visitors in the future as word gets out about this laid-back town. You'll also see a great deal of land development and real estate activity, as real estate has become an increasingly lucrative field in Todos Santos lately.

Cost of Housing: Pros

Because Todos Santos is still developing, you will be able to purchase and build on some prime real estate territory. The most expensive pieces of land are just over a million dollars, but there are many empty lots for sale near the beach that cost under $50,000 USD. Likewise, the houses for sale come at a wide price range, but with some searching, you can find a house near the beach for less than $150,000 USD. If you're in the business of real estate, you'll also find some excellent opportunities to do business.

Cost of Housing: Cons

Land development is rapidly progressing and the obscure nature of this town may not last forever. As more houses go up, the prices will increase. Housing costs aren't generally a problem; even with the prices going up, they're still fairly low.

Employment for Expats: Pros

If you're interested in flipping real estate, Todos Santos is a good place for you to set up shop, given the potential in the undeveloped land for sale. Artists and musicians will also find good company here. Artisan work is especially popular, and you'll have a fair chance of selling your wares here. If you're a martial arts or yoga instructor, there's money to be made in that as well, given the popularity of both activities.

Employment for Expats: Cons

Although there is work to be found, Todos Santos is much more of a retirement destination than it is a place to find new employment. That being said, if retirement is your goal and your interests include the arts, nature, and the varying forms of recreation this town has to offer, you won't find a finer place to settle down in your golden years.

Our Chat with a Local: Todos Santos

In Todos Santos, we chatted with Sandy, a masseuse and yoga instructor originally from San Francisco. She lives in Todos Santos during the winter months and returns to the Bay Area in the summertime, when the temperatures in Todos Santos get hot very hot.

Sandy: I've been coming back and forth to Todos Santos for almost eight years. I was a yoga instructor in the Bay Area, and I still do that. There's plenty of work if you cater to tourists. I'm divorced, and I came down here for the first time after my kids all left home and went to college.

The trip was like a reawakening for me. I spent days walking on the beach and just enjoying the atmosphere here. The cost of living is so much cheaper than the Bay Area, but the atmosphere is similar. There are lots of art and music festivals throughout the year—I always find something interesting and fun to do.

The first time I came down, I was broke, but I didn't even have to pay for housing. I got a house-sitting gig for one of the wealthier residents that only comes down a few months a year. Many people simply don't want to rent out their homes, but they also don't want to leave their properties unattended. So house sitting gigs are easy to find if you're single without pets or kids.

When I become eligible for Social Security I'll probably move down here full time and just come back to the US to visit my kids once in a while. I just love it here.

Los Barriles: A Sport Fisherman's Paradise

Looking for a place to settle down and enjoy the fruits of the sea? Look no further than the southern Baja California Sur town of Los Barriles. Here, you will find some of the best fishing and kite surfing you'll ever experience. This small town is especially famous for its marlins, but has a large variety of fish all year long. If you have a passion for sport fishing, Los Barriles has plenty to provide.

Local fishermen posing with their catch

Like many other locations in Baja California Sur, Los Barriles has a lovely mix of arid desert land and warm, sweeping coasts. The weather is warm throughout the year and has strong winds. Because of this, Los Barriles is also a popular destination for wind sports, including kite flying and wind surfing. If those things don't interest you, you can also participate in hiking, snorkeling, kayaking, mountain biking, and all sorts of other highly-active outdoor pastimes.

If your interest in local wildlife leans more toward observing instead of catching, Los Barriles has a wide variety of rare flora and fauna for you to admire. Aside from the fish, you'll also spot turtles, dolphins, rays, and even the occasional whale swimming in the warm waters. The desert has its share of interesting wildlife as well, such as the elusive Cape Pygmy Owl, making it a prime spot for birdwatching. The year-round weather is typically dry and temperate, save for the occasional tropical storm.

Los Barriles as a town dates back to the 1500s and has many historical churches, remnants of the work of missionaries who arrived with Hernan Cortez. These churches have been preserved and restored for posterity. Today, the economy of Los Barriles heavily leans on tourism and the abundant sport fishing the tourists come for. The money coming in helps provide all the conveniences and amenities of a typical city to its residents without sacrificing its easygoing atmosphere.

Whether you're looking to make a living or just take it easy, you'll be able to find it here.

The community of Los Barriles is open and welcoming to expats. About half the people living there are from another country and have flocked to this small town to make a new life. You'll have little trouble finding people who speak English here, but there's also plenty of opportunity to practice your Spanish and get to know the locals. Expats are very active in the community of Los Barriles, contributing through nonprofit groups for the betterment of students and the environment. You'll find you have plenty of options to find a place among the people here, so if you're serious about becoming part of the community, Los Barriles is one of the better options.

Location, Population and Size

Los Barriles is located on the eastern side of the Baja California Sur region, south of La Paz and North of Cabo San Lucas. It occupies the *Cabo Este* (east cape) region of southern Baja, and faces the Gulf of California, which is home to an abundant variety of ocean wildlife, including dolphins, manta rays, sea turtles, and the famous marlins. The inland, on the other hand, is mainly desert and has dozens of species of plants and animals indigenous to Baja.

A fairly small town with a relaxed atmosphere, Los Barriles has a population that's roughly divided between locals and expats living either part-time or full-time in the city. The expats are active in the community and involve themselves in local churches, scholarship programs, and extracurricular activities with the schools. It's also a popular destination for tourists who want to go fishing or participate in wind sports and you can usually see visitors fishing from boats just offshore.

Los Barriles: The Pros

Like much of the Baja California Sur region, Los Barriles takes a slow and relaxed approach to life. Many people who come here find that there's less of a rush to get things done, but that doesn't mean you won't find anything to do. If you're interested in fishing or other ocean-based hobbies, Los Barriles offers plenty of exciting options.

Fishing boats and small yachts in Los Barriles

Los Barriles is most famous for its sports fishing. Marlins are the most popular catch of the day, but you can find dorado, sailfish, snappers, roosterfish, and tuna, among many other fish.

Fishing season is at its best from May to October, but you should be able to land catches all year long. You can also try a number of different fishing techniques, such as fly fishing, deep-sea fishing, and surfcasting. If you have a competitive streak, you can participate in one of several fishing tournaments throughout the year. The coast of Los Barriles is a dream come true for anybody who's into serious sport fishing.

Besides fishing, you can also participate in wind sports, especially in the winter. One of the most exciting and popular pastimes is kiteboarding, and there are professional instructors who can teach you what you need to know.

Los Barriles: Cons

Despite fishing being one of the most popular pastimes in Los Barriles, the ocean wildlife has become increasingly at-risk due to extensive commercial fishing. There is very little enforcement on illegal fishing methods, which is having an adverse effect on the wildlife. If you intend to come to Los Barriles to enjoy the fishing, please do so responsibly.

Aside from that, the dry, arid climate lends itself to occasional power loss in homes. If you have a generator, you can avoid this, but it's still a risk to be aware of. The drinking water is generally safe, but it's still advised to use a filter or purchase bottled water for drinking.

Los Barriles lifestyle is calm and easygoing, but it's also a hotspot for fishing fanatics and people who want to participate in the wind sports. If you don't mind the crowds coming and going, you'll have no problems, but if you want to get away from the tourists, you're better off elsewhere.

Los Barriles is unique in Baja because it is also very windy. This makes it the most popular location in Baja for kite surfing and other wind sports, but the winds can be bothersome for some folks, especially in the winter, when the wind is colder and stronger.

The Weather: Pros

Los Barriles has an arid climate most of the year, despite its close proximity to the ocean. It sees less than ten inches of rainfall per year and averages between 60 to 80 degrees Fahrenheit throughout the year. If you prefer relatively warm and dry weather, you'll be perfectly happy in Los Barriles. For the most part, the weather is pleasant and consistent, though the occasional rainfall does happen. When it does, you can expect to see the desert plants bloom and flourish.

The strong winds in this town also make it an excellent spot for participating in wind sports. Los Barriles is famous for activities such as kite flying and wind surfing, especially during the winter months.

The Weather: Cons

As with any other tropical town near the ocean, you can expect to see hurricanes from time to time. Hurricane season in Los Barriles is usually during September and October. Also, while the area gets very little rain most of the year, it does see the occasional thunderstorm.

Aside from hurricanes and rainfall, there's another potential issue related to the arid climate. The dry soil and strong winds create a lot of erosion that can interrupt the supply of electricity to the town. You may have to deal with the occasional brownout or blackout as a result. If you plan to live in Los Barriles and you're concerned about losing power, the best solution is to install your own generator to combat the problem.

Once again, Los Barriles is very windy compared to the rest of Baja. This is good if you like wind sports, like kite surfing, but not so good if you dislike windy weather.

Local Population: Pros

Expats will find themselves in excellent company in Los Barriles, thanks to the town being a rather popular destination for full-time and part-time expats. Only about half the people living in Los Barriles are Mexican locals. What makes this town unique is how integrated locals and expats are here.

The expats living here are very involved with the community, contributing to churches and scholastic endeavors. Because so many people in Los Barriles are of foreign origins, you can expect the average person to speak at least some English.

Los Barriles may be a small town, but it has just about everything you'll need, including a full-sized grocery store, two banks with translators, two gas stations, a hardware store, and medical, dental, and veterinary clinics. You can also enjoy some fine dining at the local restaurants.

Local Population: Cons

If you're not interested at all in fishing or wind sports, much of the appeal of Los Barriles will be lost on you. There are certainly other activities to involve yourself in, but you'll find yourself surrounded with people engaged chiefly in those activities.

Do keep in mind that tourism is a significant source of income in Los Barriles, so you will need to learn to overlook that if tourists are not your cup of tea. Besides that, though, there aren't very many downsides to living among the local population of Los Barriles. Living here, you will find plenty of opportunities to meet and befriend both fellow expats and people who have lived in Baja their whole lives.

Cost of Housing: Pros

In Los Barriles, you can purchase certain land lots for less than $50,000 USD and a house with all the modern amenities for under $200,000 USD. Much of the property is beachfront, or at least a very short drive or walk to the ocean. Cheap beachfront property is one of the main attractions of this town, and you'll find plenty of expats who have also come here because of the low-priced housing.

It's worth noting that there are rather expensive houses for sale as well, some of which reach past the one million mark. However, these houses are truly luxury homes with huge amounts of space, prime locations, and all the amenities. If you have the money to spend on a home like this, you'll find the price is actually very reasonable compared to the cost for an equivalent luxury house elsewhere.

Cost of Housing: Cons

Because of certain issues with the water and soil conditions in Los Barriles, you will need to set aside some money for a few extra expenses you might not have to worry about elsewhere. The erosion problem tends to cause blackouts and other issues with electricity, so if you wish to avoid that, you will have to buy and maintain a generator in the event of power loss. It's also recommended that you install a good filtration system for your water, even though the cost of municipal water itself is fairly reasonable. In exchange for lower housing costs, you will need to be able to compensate for inconveniences like this. Fortunately, the costs of utilities are otherwise affordable, but make sure you don't cut corners on paying for these little extras. The cost is worth the convenience.

Employment for Expats: Pros

Los Barriles manages to strike a good balance between the remote, small-town atmosphere many people crave and the potential for making a living. Since the town is already full of expats, you'll have an easier time of finding jobs among various related businesses that already cater to tourists and expats in the area.

If you want to be involved in the community, you can also join a guild that provides scholarships to the local students. It's an excellent way to make contacts and become integrated with the community. Along with that, there's also the *Amigos de Animales*, a group that sponsors animal clinics, an organization that sets up clean-up days in Los Barriles, and even a rotary club.

There's also plenty of demand for sporting and fishing instructors, as well as tour operators.

Employment for Expats: Cons

As with any small town, job openings can be somewhat limited. While you can join one of the nonprofit organizations in order to make contacts, if you don't have plans for a job coming in, it might take a while to find work. The fortunate thing is most places in Los Barriles do have employees who speak English, but if you want to live and work there full-time, you'd best brush up on your Spanish. Aside from those limitations, you'll find Los Barriles has good potential for finding work, since many other expats are already living and working here alongside the locals.

Our Chat with a Local: Los Barriles

Paul is an avid sports fisherman and a Los Barriles local. He is originally from Oregon.

Paul: I came here for the sports fishing. Period. I liked a few other cities in Baja, but I chose Los Barriles because sports fishing is my favorite pastime and has been for the last 20 years. The fishing here is unbelievable. Whether you're trying to catch marlin or tuna, or anything else, it's here.

I loved Portland when I was growing up, but got fed up with all the newcomers coming in from other states. I felt that the city had changed completely. I was done. I had gone down to Cabo San Lucas a few times on vacation, and liked it well enough, but never considered living in Baja. Then a friend of mine told me about Los Barriles. He comes down every year to fish for marlin and one year I decided to accompany him. I caught a beautiful Blue Marlin the second day after I arrived.

I was *hooked* from that day forward—literally! [laughter].

A lot of locals offer tours and I did that in order to get to know the area better, but I pretty much knew that this was where I wanted to live right away. I practically live on my boat. And that's the way I like it.

I go back to Oregon during the winter for a few months to visit family, but I always come back to Los Barriles. Everything about my life is better here—lower blood pressure, better heath, less drinking, even. I eat a lot of my own catch and that's been one of the best health and life decisions I've ever made. It's windy, that's the only thing that bothers me sometimes, but good if you like sailing.

Mulegé: A Natural Oasis with a Lush Prehistoric History

If you are searching for a small, unique town with a rich history, look no further than Mulegé. An modern oasis built next to the *Rio Mulegé* (Mulegé River), the town is known for its fishing, robust agriculture, and many interesting historical sites. Once remote and isolated, this small town has seen a boom in tourism in recent years thanks to extensive development on the roads and the inclusion of three airstrips and an airport.

Long considered a prime location to live, the aboriginal peoples of Mexico built their settlements near the Rio Mulegé to reap the benefits of the fresh water. To this day, a cave system in the nearby Sierra de Guadalupe Mountains filled with paintings and petroglyphs still remains, carefully preserved by the locals. You can get a tour guide to take you there and teach you all about the ancient peoples who made the paintings.

Santa Rosalía de Mulegé, a historical mission site, is also located in the town. The mission dates back to the early 1700s. It's a popular point of interest, but even that pales in comparison to perhaps the most fascinating aspect of Mulegé's history, the state penitentiary museum.

The town of Mulegé boasts the unique claim of having a barless prison. Rather than locking people up, the prisoners were permitted to roam the town during the day, going about their work and even having families. The only condition was that they return to their cells by 6 PM. This honor system was used to motivate prisoners to keep each other in check; escapees would be tracked down and returned by their fellow prisoners in order to ensure they maintained their relative freedom.

Today, the prison now serves as a museum to educate people on the unique Baja culture of this town, and the neighborly attitude of the people that made this prison a possibility endures to this day.

Mulegé is regarded as an especially hospitable and welcoming town. Tourists flock here to see the historical sites, enjoy the fishing, and spend time on the nearby shores. You'll have an easy time of finding people among the locals who are fluent in English, and with nine different restaurants, you'll be able to enjoy a variety of local cuisine.

Day-to-day living is mellow and friendly. The weather is warm year-round and the excellent fishing and agricultural industry is one of the major appeals of living here. Mulegé is particularly famous for its mangos, which flourish in this oasis environment. Although a small town, fishing, agriculture, and tourism have made this place very prosperous. You'll find life here welcoming and comfortable. If you're looking for a place with a warm atmosphere and rich history, Mulegé is perfect for you.

Location, Population and Size

The small town of Mulegé, located on the eastern shores of Baja California Sur, is unique among the many small towns populating Baja California Sur. While most of the region consists of desert, Mulegé is an oasis settled right on the *Rio Mulegé*. It's close to the Gulf of California and has a number of interesting geological features, most notably the painting and petroglyph-filled cave systems and peaceful swimming coves.

The town has a small population; it's only the fourth-largest city in the Mulegé Municipality. However, its location and plentiful water source makes it a pleasant place to live. Since rain is rare in Baja California Sur, the river-source water is a boon to Mulegé, sustaining a host of tropical crops. You can expect to see a lot of farming and fishing activity in this town. It's also popular tourist attraction for eco-tourists who want to observe local wildlife.

Mulegé: The Pros

Mulegé has a number of interesting qualities that make it unique among the towns and cities of Baja California Sur. If you want to live someplace that's unlike the other areas of Baja, this is certainly a worthwhile contender.

Perhaps the biggest draw is its fascinating history. This area has long been populated by people because of the natural irrigation the river provides. In the past, the economy depended mainly on fishing and agriculture, and both of those things are still important today. The town is sure to catch the eye of any history buffs. The carefully-preserved 1705 mission, *Santa Rosalía de Mulegé*, and the penitentiary museum are also particularly noteworthy.

Mulegé is a small town, but for its size, has a relatively strong economy built on its fishing, crops, and many visitors who want to experience the rare and fascinating features of the area. It has the attitude of a small town, yet features five famous hotels.

The unique weather and lush flora also makes Mulegé an attractive place to settle down. Fishing, water activities, and the nearby beaches are all considered major draws. In order to accommodate visitors, the town has several hotels and restaurants. The town is also noted for its mangos, which grow well in the warm, humid environment, and many restaurants feature the fruits in their dishes.

Mulegé: Cons

The river is indeed a boon to the agriculture of Mulegé, but it can be treacherous during the stormy seasons. Mulegé is prone to flooding and has more than its fair share of hurricane damage. If you live in Mulegé, you have to be very attentive to weather reports.

Buying housing can be a real challenge here. This town is notably hospitable toward its guests, but because so many people are attracted to this town, finding a place to live has become difficult. The houses posted online for sale tend to be snatched up quickly. It's much easier to come here as a temporary visitor than it is as a new permanent resident. A good idea is to visit the town for an extended period and decide if the area is right for you, then consider renting for a while until your perfect "forever home" becomes available.

The Weather: Pros

Mulegé is situated around a freshwater stream, one of the few true rivers in Baja California Sur, which feeds into an estuary. While other cities and towns in Baja California Sur tend to be primarily arid desert land, Mulegé is a natural oasis with plenty of water. If you're not a fan of arid climates but still want to live in the Baja region, this is a choice location for you.

As with the rest of the area, Mulegé is a temperate tropical zone, so you can expect the weather to be warm throughout the year. The temperature rarely dips below 60 degrees Fahrenheit, even in the middle of winter. During the summer, the weather is generally in the low-to-mid 90s.

The Weather: Cons

This may be good news for people who don't like dry weather, but do be aware that if you move to Mulegé, you will see more than your fair share of humidity. This oasis town has a great deal of moisture in the air all year, so expect to see lots of considerably muggy days during the summer.

Just like the rest of Baja California Sur, Mulegé experiences its share of hurricanes, but its proximity to the river compounds the problem in ways the more arid parts of Baja don't usually have to worry about. Mulegé is prone to flooding after major storms, so water damage is a very real possibility. It also tends to suffer property damage of all kinds especially during hurricanes. While hurricanes in any part of BCS are no joke, they tend to hit this town harder than most, so if you live here, take hurricane warnings very seriously.

Local Population: Pros

The people of Mulegé are welcoming and laid-back, and they are widely regarded as showing excellent hospitality to newcomers. The legacy of such a cooperative community that even the prisoners do their part still remains in this quiet town, and there is plenty to do if you have an appreciation for the history here.

The locals are protective of their historical sites and have taken precautions to avoid potential defacing or vandalism. As a result, you need to contact the guide in order to see the caves with the paintings and petroglyphs, perhaps the most spectacular and historically remarkable site Mulegé has to offer. Most guides are quite amiable to showing visitors and new residents around, being very knowledgeable about the area and also speaking fluent

English. The penitentiary museum, another place of great interest, does not require a guide, though there is a recommended donation. Much like the historical prison itself, it relies on the honor system and good intentions of the people in the town.

Local Population: Cons

The cons of living here are largely subjective when it comes to the locals. Mulegé is regarded as a very hospitable town, so whether this place suits you really depends more on how much you like the quiet life. If a small-town lifestyle isn't for you, chances are you might find Mulegé to be a little dull. Although the tourism industry is a large part of the economy, there isn't quite so much activity as some of the larger towns and cities. There really aren't a lot of drawbacks to the local population if you're looking for a place to live that's quiet and out of the way, but expats looking for a more exciting life will be better off trying somewhere else.

Cost of Housing: Pros

Property in Mulegé tends to have a low price for the most part, whether it's a land lot or an already-furnished house. Much of the land for sale costs less than $100,000 USD, which is an incredible bargain for such coveted territory. There are a few pieces of property here and there that have a truly astronomical cost, but these are usually large compounds more comparable to mansions than houses. There are certainly smaller houses and condos within a reasonable price range, though you will need to do a lot of research and hunting to find one.

If you so wish, you may also choose to forgo purchasing or renting a house and instead try living in one of the RV parks. These parks provide most of the utilities you need, though keep in mind that electricity may be limited to the 30-watt level.

Cost of Housing: Cons

Property in Mulegé may be relatively inexpensive, but it's also becoming scarce. Such is the price you pay when setting your sights on living in an oasis along the coast. Many of the houses you will find on real estate websites have already been sold. The houses you do find for sale are often rentals in disguise. Be very careful to make note of what the fine print says on any contract you sign. Because of its appeal and popularity as a destination for both expats and tourists, you may have no choice but to rent, but be wary of possible scams or deceptive rental agreements.

Employment for Expats: Pros

The biggest industry for Mulegé is historical and archeological-based tourism, and it is slowly becoming more and more well-known internationally for its fishing, beaches, and historical sites. If you happen to speak fluent English, you may find yourself well-suited for working with tourists who need an English-speaking guide. The many hotels and restaurants likewise may have a place for you, as hospitality is of great importance in this town.

Employment for Expats: Cons

Simply put, Mulegé just isn't as much of an expat destination as some of the other places in this book. It's certainly not impossible to find a job, but there are fewer opportunities here. You may have a hard time looking for work in such a small town. Once again, the importance of the tourism industry here means you will probably have a good chance of finding work in that field, especially since many tourists will prefer somebody who can speak English. But if you're looking to truly be a part of the authentic Baja fabric, having to work with tourists every day can feel like a bit of a farce.

Loreto: Safety, Community, and Old World Grace and Charm

Loreto is the oldest settlement in all of Baja California Sur. Founded in 1697 by Jesuit missionaries, this city has a deep history that goes all the way back to its aboriginal people, who had settled the area and left behind cave paintings in the nearby *Sierra de la Giganta* Mountains. Today, several missions, some of which are still in use, can be found in Loreto. The people here take great pride in their history and celebrate a number of festivals each year.

Sports are an important pastime in this city and many people enjoy participating in them. Every September, people get together for the Loreta 400, an off-road race through the desert. This city also has three fishing tournaments, one of which puts all the proceeds toward charity. Golf, water sports, diving, and swimming are also popular. If you're an active, competitive individual, you'll find plenty of things to do in this town.

Loreto has some magnificent beaches and local fresh seafood is held in high regard. Several varieties of ocean fish, including tuna, dorado, and snappers, can be caught and prepared locally throughout the year. Chocolate clams also abound in Loreto and feature prominently in seafood establishments. In many restaurants, if you bring your catch to them, their chefs will prepare it for you.

Much effort in Loreto goes into preserving what makes it special, whether it's the historical sites or just the natural beauty of the region. Likewise, the locals take the preservation of their culture seriously. Loreto welcomes tourists who want to enjoy the shores or participate in eco-tours to spot grey whales.

However, Loreto residents do not want their city to become another Cabo. Rather than trying to meet the expectations of foreign visitors, the people here place great importance on preserving their culture and allowing other people the chance to appreciate it.

One of the most notable qualities of Loreto is how safe it is. In general, Baja California Sur is one of the safest areas in the entire country of Mexico, and Loreto is widely regarded as being one of the safest cities. Violent crime is very rare and the people here are quite friendly with each other. The majority of them are extended family and they take that relational bond seriously. Loreto drinking water is also known for being especially clean and people drink from the tap with no problems.

Loreto is one of the more genuine coastal towns you can find to settle down in, though it will take some adjusting to become part of the community and get used to the different culture. It's very important that you be willing to learn Spanish if you decide to live here. The cost of living is slightly higher than many other places in Baja, as well. But if you're looking for a place to stay that's extremely safe, genuine, friendly, and full of interesting history, you won't find a better destination.

Location, Population and Size

Loreto is located on the eastern coast of Baja California Sur. It is somewhat remote from surrounding cities, but access to this city is easy thanks to the highway and international airport. Loreto has a moderate population of around 15,000 people, as well as a somewhat active tourism industry. It's by far the largest city in the Loreto Municipality; in fact, it's the only city, as all other towns in the area have fewer than 300 people living in them.

Loreto is bordered by the Gulf of California, the Sierra de la Giganta Mountains, and a large dry creek bed known as the *Arroyo Letto*, which usually only has water following heavy rainfall. The Transpeninsular Highway meets the western side of the city, which is what makes Loreto a fairly easy place to visit, despite being geographically isolated from the few surrounding towns in the Loreto Municipality.

Loreto: The Pros

Loreto is famed for its close community, safety, long history, and variety of beautiful landscapes. From the towering mountains of Sierra de la Giganta and the dry *Arroyo Letto* creek to the warm, sandy coast, you can find a little bit of everything in the scenery.

Loreto is the oldest Spanish settlement in Baja and has plenty of interesting sights from its colonial history, including the *Misión San Francisco Javier de Viggé-Biaundó*, which is still in use and is considered the best-preserved mission on the peninsula. In the mountains, you can find cave paintings made by the indigenous people who settled in the area long before the Spanish arrived. Today, many people come to visit these sites and they are a significant aspect of the local culture.

Perhaps one of the most notable things about Loreto is how safe is it. Loreto is regarded as not only one of the safest places in Baja, but in the entire country of Mexico. The crime rate is very low, even for minor crimes such as petty theft, and there is 24-hour security in the city. The tap water in Loreto is regarded as exceptionally clean. If safety is your biggest worry, Loreto will put most of these worries at ease.

Loreto: Cons

Despite being a tourist hotspot, it's not a place where you can expect to find a lot of fellow expats living full-time. Loreto has a lot of good qualities, but this city is not as welcoming to permanent expats. On the bright side, if you really want to get away and have a life that is the antithesis of Cabo's wild nightlife, you will enjoy Loreto.

You can truly immerse yourself in local Mexican culture here. However, be sure you are able to handle the change before you consider moving here. Make sure you speak Spanish, because you'll find that many people living here do not speak English.

The other possible drawbacks are the weather and cost of living. The weather more humid than you'll find elsewhere in Baja, which otherwise tends to be an arid climate. This means you'll find more lush greenery but also more mosquitos. It's also a bit more costly to live in Loreto than it is in some of the other coastal towns in Baja. It's still less expensive than the typical cost of living in any coastal area in the United States, however.

The Weather: Pros

If you want someplace nice and warm to live, Loreto will not disappoint. The temperature is above 60 Fahrenheit no matter which season you are in. You'll be able to enjoy warm water throughout the year. Loreto has a storm season, but even so, most days will be nice and sunny.

If you enjoy activities such as kite flying or wind surfing, you'll be able to do that here thanks to the ocean breeze. The best time for this is typically during autumn or winter, which are the windiest months.

The Weather: Cons

The weather in Loreto is hot and humid throughout the year, which can be hard to adjust to for anybody who is used to cooler or dryer weather. Even during the winter months, the temperature tends to average in the mid-60s, and summers usually stay in the 90s. Sometimes the summer temperatures climb into the triple-digits. The humidity level in Loreto is above 60 all year long.

As always, be on the lookout for hurricanes, as they will be a threat on any tropical coast. Hurricane season runs from June to November and brings with it heavy rainfall and also occasional flooding.

Local Population: Pros

Loreto is a bit larger than most of the coastal towns of Baja California Sur, though not quite as big and crowded as La Paz or Los Cabos. Loreto is the oldest settlement established by the Spanish in the entire Baja California Sur region. Because of this, the people here take pride in their long history. Before the arrival of the Spanish, many indigenous people had made their homes in the region and some remnants of their settlements can still be seen today.

Loreto is a generally neighborly place that puts great importance on family. People here do their best to maintain a peaceful lifestyle. Violent crimes of any kind are very rare and are met with immediate action. The neighborly attitude of Loreto extends outside the borders of its city; it maintains an active relationship with a number of cities in southern California and around Los Angeles, including Hermosa Beach, Cerritos, and Ventura.

Sports and other active pastimes are a big part of the culture here. You can expect to see tournaments and celebrations of sports during festivals, particularly during the *Feast of Our Lady of Loreto*, which is held on the eighth of September. In addition, they also celebrate with music, dancing, and exhibitions.

Local Population: Cons

Loreto has a somewhat low immigration rate compared to other cities and towns in Baja California Sur. If you choose to expatriate here, you will need to put concentrated effort into knowing the language and being able to understand the culture. Speaking only English and generally refusing to assimilate with the locals will greatly work against you here. While this place is a tourist attraction, it's not usually a destination for expats and it will take time to adjust to the new way of life, but if you're looking for a major change of pace, you'll find it here.

It is worth noting that there are many large extended families living in Loreto. While this is not necessarily a con, you should keep it in mind. You can expect to meet a lot of people here who happen to be related. Family is considered important in Loreto, so take extra care in being respectful of this mindset.

Cost of Housing: Pros

If you're looking to live in a rental house or apartment, you can find many nice places to live that are right on the beach or very close to it for between $1,000 and $1,500 USD per month. Considering the cost you would normally pay to rent such property in other countries, this is a fairly inexpensive arrangement.

Cost of Housing: Cons

While the cost of living is lower than it would be in places like the United States, Loreto does have a somewhat higher cost of living compared to most other locations in Mexico, since many resources in this city need to be imported from mainland Mexico. Expect to pay somewhere around $1,200 per month or more for day-to-day living. As for the cost of houses, most are over $200,000 or even $300,000 USD, though you can find a house or two that costs less. Even undeveloped lots can cost more than the ones for sale in smaller towns.

Employment for Expats: Pros

Since Loreto is a bit larger than some of the small coastal towns, there is more room for local employment here than you might find elsewhere. Tourism, as always, is a major industry and you can also find work in that. Conservation and other eco-friendly activities are also very important to the Loreto lifestyle and getting involved can help you make contacts in order to find ways to be part of the community and make a living.

Fishing is a big part of life in Loreto, so if you're interested in making your living from the sea, you can take part in that. Chocolate clams, tuna, and dorado are all prized catches here. If you're more interested in education, there are dozens of schools you can look into, ranging from kindergarten all the way to college level, complete with bachelor's programs. Many schools offer bilingual education, which is always an opportunity for those who speak both languages fluently.

Employment for Expats: Cons

You must learn to speak Spanish if you truly want to do well for yourself here. Although its status as a tourist destination ensures you will always find some people who speak English, since this is not a major immigration city, you will have more trouble than usual if you speak only English. If you're not willing to put in the work to adapt to the local culture in Loreto, you're going to have a very difficult time fitting in. If that's the case, you might be better off moving to a city with a larger population of expats.

Reference Information for Local Schools

Education

For families looking to move to Baja California Sur, one of the crucial factors in deciding where to move is the quality of the educational institutions in the area. To help you with your decision, we have compiled a number of noteworthy schools from the different towns and cities outlined in this book.

Note: In most Mexican schools, both public or private, school uniforms are mandatory.

Schools in La Paz

There are many educational opportunities in La Paz. Public schools, bilingual private schools, language schools, vocational schools, and modern universities are all available in the area. The expat population in La Paz is only about 6,000 out of 250,000 people, so it may be more difficult to find information regarding these schools on the internet in English.

We found that it was easier to find information about educational institutions through Facebook. If you are researching schools, try searching "schools in La Paz, Baja California Sur" in the Facebook search bar and a number of schools will pop up. We also suggest connecting with other expats (TripAdvisor has several excellent forums) and asking them about the schools in the area, since information on the internet is limited. Here are a few of the schools we found in La Paz.

Instituto Bilingüe Del Valle

Address: Belisario Domínguez 3510 Esq. Oaxaca Col. Pueblo Nuevo
Phone: (612) 125 3417
Contact Page: http://www.ibv.edu.mx/contacto.aspx
Website: http://www.ibv.edu.mx/index.aspx
Facebook: https://www.facebook.com/IBVLaPaz
Education Levels: elementary and middle school

Instituto Bilingüe Del Valle (IBV) is a bilingual school that educates elementary and middle school-aged children. The school prides itself on its use of technology in teaching students, its small class sizes, its foreign language courses, and its commitment to improving students' thinking skills.

Colegio Bilingüe Maria Fernanda

Address: Campus Melitón—Melitón Albañez e/ Puebla y Sinaloa Col. Las Garzas, La Paz, B.C.S.
Campus Cuauhtémoc—Cuauhtémoc no. 1615 Col. Adolfo Ruíz Cortinez, La Paz, B.C.S.
Website: http://colegiomariafernanda.com/index.html
Facebook: https://www.facebook.com/colegiomariafernanda
Education Levels: elementary, middle school, high school

Colegio Bilingüe Maria Fernanda is another bilingual school that offers comprehensive education for students from preschool through high school. This school also offers extracurricular activities. Their goal is to prepare students for their future by educating them in a safe and loving learning environment.

Instituto Mar de Cortés

Address: Calle desierto de Sonora S/N esq. Prolongación J. Mújica, Fraccionamiento Villas de San Lorenzo, C.P. 23085
Phone: (612) 123.22.02

Website: http://www.institutomardecortes.edu.mx/
Facebook: https://www.facebook.com/InstMardeCortes/
Education Levels: high school

Instituto Mar de Cortés is a high school located in La Paz. This school's goal is to educate future leaders by providing them with a comprehensive education and giving them the tools needed to have a successful career. The school also partners with other educational institutions to provide the best learning experience they can for their students.

Colegio de Bachilleres (COBACH) del Estado de Baja California Sur

Address: Sierra de las Vírgenes y Bordo de Contención, Col. 8 de Octubre
Phone: (612) 121-1801
Website: http://www.cobachbcs.edu.mx/
Facebook: https://www.facebook.com/cobachbcsmx
Education Levels: high school

This is another high school committed not only to provide a great education for its students, but also to help them develop into citizens who will have a positive impact on the world. This school also has campuses in Los Cabos, Mulegé, and Loreto.

El Nopal Spanish-Language School

Address: Legaspy Street #1885 / Yucatán and Padre Kino. La Paz B.C.S
Phone: +52 (612) 177-4098
Contact Page: http://www.elnopalspanish.com/contact.php
Email: info@elnopalspanish.com
Website: http://www.elnopalspanish.com/
Facebook: https://www.facebook.com/El-Nopal-Spanish-493621814002781/

El Nopal takes a practical approach to learning a new language. Students can participate in different activities that will allow them to learn and speak Spanish in ways they are likely to encounter in everyday life. Some activities offered through *El Nopal* include cooking classes, visits to local markets, volunteer work, and a homestay with local Mexican families.

Conalep

Address: Antonio Álvarez Rico esquina con Lorenzo Núñez Avilés Col. Emiliano Zapata La Paz, Baja California Sur
Phone: +52 (612) 125-1137
Website: http://www.conalepbcs.edu.mx/
Facebook:https://www.facebook.com/conaleplapaz/?rf=31373 2438780612
Educational Levels: high school

Conalep is a vocational high school designed to prepare students for the workforce or to continue their studies at a university. Conalep offers General Nursing, Tourism and Hospitality, Industrial Electricity, and Food and Drink courses to its students.

Universidad Autónoma de Baja California Sur (UABCS)

Address: Carretera al Sur KM 5.5., Apartado Postal 19-,B, C.P. 23080, La Paz Baja California Sur, México
Phone: (612) 12 388 00
Website: http://uabcs.mx/inicio
Facebook:https://www.facebook.com/UniversidadAutonomade BajaCaliforniaSur/

The Autonomous University of Baja California Sur is a public university with departments in the following fields of study:

- Animal Science and Habitat Conservation
- Earth Sciences
- Marine and Coastal Sciences
- Fisheries Engineering
- Computer Systems
- Social Sciences and Law
- Economics
- Humanities

Centro Interdisciplinario de Ciencias Marinas (CICIMAR)

Address: Av. Instituto Politécnico Nacional s/n Col. Playa Palo de Santa Rita Apdo. Postal 592. Código Postal 23096 La Paz, B.C.S.
Phone: +52 (612) 123-4658
Contact Page: http://www.ipn.mx/Paginas/Contacto.aspx
Website: http://www.cicimar.ipn.mx/Paginas/Inicio.aspx
Facebook: https://www.facebook.com/ipn.mx/

The *Centro Interdisciplinario de Ciencias Marinas del Instituto Politécnico Nacional* (CICIMAR-IPN) is a public university that focuses on developing scientific and technological research in the marine sciences.

Its four departments are Fisheries and Marine Biology, Technology Development, Oceanography, and Plankton and Marine ecology. CICIMAR offers a master's degree in Marine Resources Management and a doctorate in Marine Sciences.

Centro de Investigación Biológica del Noreste (CIBNOR)

Address: Km 1 Carretera a San Juan de la Costa "El Comitán" La Paz, BCS 23201, Mexico
Phone: +52 (612) 123 8484
Website: http://www.cibnor.gob.mx/
Facebook: https://www.facebook.com/cibnor/

CIBNOR is primarily a research university whose goal is to improve society through scientific research, technological innovation, and promoting sustainability. This institution provides masters and doctorate degrees in Aquaculture, Sustainable Agriculture, Marine Biology, Ecology, and Fisheries.

Schools in Cabo San Lucas
Colegio Amaranto International School

Address: Km. 6.7 Carretera Transpeninsular s/n Col. El Tezal C.P. 23454 Cabo San Lucas, B.C.S México
Phone: +52 (624) 145-8700
Contact Page: http://amaranto.edu.mx/en/contact-us/
Website: http://amaranto.edu.mx/es/
Facebook: https://www.facebook.com/ColegioAmaranto
Education Levels: Smart Start (nursery), preschool, elementary

Founded in 1996, *Colegio Amaranto* is a bilingual international school committed to recognizing and building the individual talents of their students, as well as strengthening their interpersonal skills.

Amaranto was the first school in Mexico to use a SMART Board in all of their interactive classrooms. This technology gives students a more interactive learning experience and develops their digital skills. The "Infoteca" builds students' research skills while promoting personal responsibility in the learning process. The institution also believes in promoting student's physical health through nutritious food and physical education classes.

Amaranto's English specialists use various teaching methods supported by the Common Core standards and the Common European Framework of Reference to make sure students gain the confidence to speak and write in a second language on a variety of subjects. Sixth graders also have the opportunity to participate in an international exchange by visiting the sister school "Charlotte Country Day School" in North Carolina.

Colegio El Camino

Address: Callejón del Jorongo 210, Col. El Pedregal, Cabo San Lucas, B.C.S. Mexico
Phone: +52 (624) 143-2100
Contact Page: http://elcamino.edu.mx/contact-us
Website: http://elcamino.edu.mx/
Facebook: https://www.facebook.com/colegioelcaminio
Education Levels: nursery, preschool, elementary, middle school, high school

Colegio El Camino is a private K-12, nonsectarian, nonprofit organization civil association. There are currently 350 students. Most of the students are Mexican citizens, but there are also many international families. El Camino enjoys international accreditation with both AdvancED and the International Baccalaureate Diploma Program. They are registered with the *Secretaría de Educación Pública (SEP)* and they are currently a candidate school with the International Baccalaureate Primary Years Program.

El Camino's goal is to develop students' ability to think critically instead of memorizing and reciting facts. Their bilingual program begins at the nursery stage. El Camino also provides counseling and career planning. They also have agreements with several Mexican universities for high-performing students.

Colegio LICEO / Colegio Papalotl

Address: Campus Centro: 5 de Febrero e/l Zaragoza y M. Ocampo Col Ejidal Cabo San Lucas, BCS
Campus Tezal: Fracc. 1A Y1B acceso Ppal, del Tezal Col Tezal, Cabo San Lucas, BCS
Phone: (624) 143-1636 Campus Centro
Contact Page: http://www.liceoloscabos.edu.mx/contacto
Website: http://www.liceoloscabos.edu.mx

Facebook: https://www.facebook.com/colegiopapalotl
Education Levels: nursery, elementary, middle school, high school

Colegio LICEO is a bilingual educational institution committed to developing future leaders capable of improving their own communities and society at large. Educational programs offered at LICEO include constructive mathematics, music, art, physical education, extracurricular activities, and an after-school program. LICEO hires highly-qualified staff and uses cutting-edge technology on its campus. There are also security cameras and nursing facilities on campus to keep students safe and healthy.

Colegio Peninsula

Address: Vista al Mar S/N Fracc. Brisas del Pacífico, Cabo San Lucas, BCS
Phone: (624) 105-0565 / (624) 146-4117 / (624) 143-3088
Email: colegiopeninsula@hotmail.com
admisiones@colegiopeninsula.edu.mx
Website: www.colegiopeninsula.edu.mx
Facebook: https://www.facebook.com/cole.peninsula
Education Levels: preschool, elementary, middle school

Colegio Peninsula is equipped with a highly-trained staff and adequate facilities for different educational levels, including laboratories, library, recreation areas, cafeteria, and more. *Colegio Peninsula* has joined with the UNO International system, a program based on developing thinking skills. In partnership with Animal Planet, *Colegio Peninsula* uses educational software to improve students' knowledge in both Spanish and English and the school makes use of iPads for technical support. *Colegio Peninsula* also has an English certification from the University of Cambridge.

Delmar International School

Address: Paseo del Sol, El Tezal, Cabo San Lucas, Baja California Sur. CP: 23454
Phone: (624) 131 5002 / (624) 105 9357
Email: info@delmarschool.edu.mx
Website: http://www.delmarschool.edu.mx/
Facebook: https://www.facebook.com/delmarschool/
Education Levels: preschool, elementary, middle school, high school

Delmar International School is a bilingual institution that focuses on academic excellence and creating future leaders to make a better society. According to Delmar's website, the institution is inspired by a "Christian vision of life, aimed at promoting personal growth through the practice of moral virtues". The campus also has many modern facilities including smart classrooms, a robotics workshop, and an Olympic-sized swimming pool.

Instituto Baldor

Address: Carretera Transpeninsular KM.7.7 Cabo San Lucas, B.C.S.
Phone: (624) 104-3700
Email: direccion_general@institutobaldor.edu.mx
Website: www.institutobaldor.edu.mx
Education Levels: elementary, middle school, high school

Founded in 2004, *Instituto Baldor* is committed to developing the intellectual and social skills of its students so that they will grow up to be leaders in creating a better future. Students are taught to respect one another regardless of social status or religious beliefs. Baldor has a diverse student body and the school honors this diversity by celebrating various holidays.

Baldor was one of the first schools in the area to offer an MBA tourism management program because Los Cabos is a favorite for tourists visiting Mexico. Students have also won first place in Science, Physics, Chemistry, and Mathematics competitions.

Instituto Peninsular

Address: Carretera Transpeninsular Km. 6.5 S/N. Col. El Tezal
Cabo San Lucas 23410
Phone: (624) 104-3454
Website:
http://institutopeninsular.edu.mx/principal/INICIO.html
Facebook:
https://www.facebook.com/InstitutoPeninsularOficial
Education Levels: middle school, high school

Instituto Peninsular's goal is help shape young people into becoming spiritually strong, technical, and scientific adults that will have a positive impact locally and globally. Peninsular provides tutoring, a library with tech consultations, and science labs. *Instituto Peninsular* is sponsored by the Letty Coppel Foundation and associated with the Monterrey Institute of Technology and Higher Education.

Instituto Samarin

Address: Narciso Mendoza No. 2708 esq. Álvaro Obregón Col.
Juárez C.P. 23469
Phone: (624) 143-3169 / (624) 143-2017
Email: relacionespublicas@institutosamarin.com
Website: http://www.institutosamarin.com/index.html
Facebook: https://www.facebook.com/instituto.samarin
Education Levels: nursery, preschool, elementary

Instituto Samarin supports the academic and personal development of its students through highly-qualified instructors, bilingual education, a positive school community, modern technology, and cultural and artistic activities.

Schools in San José del Cabo
Centro Escolar Picacho (Colegio McGregor)

Address: Colegios en Los Cabos. Carretera Transpeninsular km 24.8 col Cerro Colorado, San José del Cabo, Baja California Sur. Código Postal 23400.
Phone: +52 (624) 144-5595
Email: info@cepicacho.edu.mx
Website: www.cepicacho.edu.mx
Facebook: https://www.facebook.com/pages/Centro-Escolar-Picacho/509583065802629
Education Levels: preschool, elementary, middle school, high school

With over twenty years of experience, Centro Escolar Picacho is an educational institution that prides itself on the bilingual and multicultural education it provides to its students. Picacho has foreign and Mexican national instructors committed to providing a high level of academic training, promoting human, social, intellectual and transcendent values, and developing critical thinking skills. Centro Escolar Picacho thinks locally and globally by educating students with the hopes of building a better country and having a positive impact on the world in general.

Colegio Alebrije

Address: Guadalupe Victoria s/n (entre Vicente Guerrero y Francisco I. Madero) Col. San José Viejo, San José del Cabo, Baja California Sur, Mexico C.P. 23437
Phone: (624) 146-0252
Email: direccion@colegioalebrije.com
Website: http://colegioalebrije.com/index.html

Facebook: https://www.facebook.com/Alebrije.Colegio/
Education Levels: nursery, preschool, elementary, middle school

Colegio Alebrije is a bilingual institution committed to the intellectual, cultural, technological, and moral growth of its students. Programs offered at Colegio Alebrije include English, physical education, music, art, ecology, and human development.

Uniforms are required for all students, but can be bought on campus along with books and supplies. Alebrije also has a lot of green areas and modern facilities, and every classroom is spacious and air conditioned.

Colegio Ugarte de Los Cabos

Address: Calle Julia Navarrete y Guerrero No. 1430 Colonia Mauricio Castro, San José del Cabo C.P.23400 B.C.S.
Phone: (624) 142-6235 / (624) 142-0935
Contact Page: http://www.colegiougarte.net/contacto.html
Website: http://www.colegiougarte.net/index.html
Facebook: https://www.facebook.com/colegiougartteloscabos
Education Levels: elementary, middle school, high school

Colegio Ugarte de Los Cabos is an educational community that promotes Christian humanist ideals forging leaders with high academic standards and social conscience to respond to current and future challenges through transforming their environment in a positive way. On their shield are the words "order, work, joy" and they use these values in their facilities and the way they educate children.

Montessori Regina

Address: Nicolas Tamaral, Lote 5. Mza. 8, 3 blocks from Kinesis Gym, Col. Chamizal || San José del Cabo, B.C.S.
Phone: (624) 146-9401
Email: info@montessoriregina.com
Website: http://montessoriregina.com/en
Education Levels: preschool, bilingual elementary

Montessori Regina is the first Montessori preschool and elementary school established in the city of San José del Cabo. Montessori education is an educational approach developed by Italian physician and educator Maria Montessori characterized by an emphasis on independence, freedom within limits, and respect for a child's natural psychological, physical, and social development.

Montessori Regina works with children aged 1.5 to 6 years old.

Schools in Todos Santos
The Sierra School of Todos Santos

Phone: (52) 612-202-6142
Contact Page: http://www.sierraschool.org/contact.html
Email: contact@sierraschool.org
Website: http://www.sierraschool.org/
Facebook: https://www.facebook.com/The-Sierra-School-of-Todos-Santos-1579631475654487/
Education Levels: high school

The Sierra School of Todos Santos, a Mexican Civic Association and a French non-profit organization, is an educational project for Mexican and international youth in Todos Santos, BCS, Mexico, seeking SEP and International

Baccalaureate Diploma Program (IB DP) accreditation as a secondary school program. The schools offers a rigorous and challenging English and Spanish course of study in the humanities, literature, math, art, ecology, sustainability, and sports.

Escuela Pacífica

Address: Escuela Pacifica Col. San Vicente Todos Santos, BCS, Mexico
Phone: 612.156.5309
Contact Page:
http://www.escuelapacifica.org/Escuela_Pacifica/Contact_Us.html
Website:http://www.escuelapacifica.org/Escuela_Pacifica/Welcome.html
Education Levels: elementary

Escuela Pacífica (EP) is a unique learning opportunity for children in first through sixth grade in the Todos Santos area. EP creates multicultural bilingual intimate classroom settings that offer a joyful interdisciplinary approach to motivate lifelong learning. EP utilizes community involvement and sustainability to create and inspire productive global citizens.

Colorado State University Todos Santos, BCS

Address: CSU Todos Santos Center Ciruelos Entre Carretera Transpeninsular y Tamarindos Todos Santos Municipio de La Paz B.C.S 23300 Mexico
Email: csutodossantos@colostate.edu
Phone: 612-145-0687
Contact Page: http://todossantos.colostate.edu/contact-us/
Website: http://todossantos.colostate.edu/
Facebook: https://www.facebook.com/CSUTodosSantos

CSU Todos Santos Center is an international outpost of Colorado State University. The Center is an opportunity for CSU students to grow as global citizens in their understanding of and appreciation for other cultures; the Center provides a variety of research and educational opportunities that CSU students would not otherwise be able to be a part of. The Center also creates a community hub for educational sessions and information sharing.

Schools in Mulegé
COBACH Mulegé, BCS

Address: Av. Prof. Carlos Moreno Preciado s/n, Colonia Magisterial
Phone: (615) 152-0097
Website: http://www.cobachbcs.edu.mx/
Facebook: https://www.facebook.com/cobachbcsmx

Colegio México

Address: Colonia Centro, Guerrero Negro, Mulegé, Baja California Sur, C.P. 23940
Phone: +01 (615) 157-0161
Education Levels: elementary, middle school, high school

This is a primary and secondary school. Keep in mind, there are multiple schools with this name, so be careful not to confuse one for the other.

Schools in Loreto
COBACH Loreto, BCS

Address: Fco. I. Madero Esq. Calle Preparatoria, Colonia El Jaral
Phone: (613) 135-0054
Website: http://www.cobachbcs.edu.mx/

Facebook: https://www.facebook.com/cobachbcsmx

UABCS Campus Loreto

Address: Boulevard Paseo Ugarte y tamaral Col. Centro
Loreto, Baja California Sur
Phone: 135-1826
Email: cposadas@uabcs.mx
Website: http://www.uabcsloreto.com/2016/
Facebook: https://www.facebook.com/Uabcs-Loreto-1703802339869286/

The UABCS University at the Loreto campus has contributed to training professionals to create solutions to problems in the social environment, and to create leaders with academic excellence and a high sense of ethical, social, and environmental responsibility.

About the *Expat Fever* Series

Are you ready for a major lifestyle change? The *Expat Fever* Series is all about the demystifying the expat journey. If you want to start fresh in a new country and immerse yourself in a new culture but aren't sure where to start, our books are packed with information that should help put you on the right path.

Our books are meant to give readers a sense of what it's really like to live in a specific area, and all of them include candid interviews with real expats, who discuss both the pros and the cons of their expat journey.

Is expatriating right for you? Learn more about our series and sign up for alerts at: *www.expatfever.com.*